GOD
WANTS A
RELATIONSHIP
WITH YOU!

BRUCE GEARY

ISBN 978-1-64468-947-9 (Paperback)
ISBN 978-1-64468-948-6 (Digital)

Stories based on and scripture quotations from The Holy Bible,
English Standard Version® (ESV®) unless otherwise noted.

Covenant Books, Inc.
11661 Hwy 707
Murrells Inlet, SC 29576
www.covenantbooks.com

CONTENTS

ACKNOWLEDGEMENTS

I would like to thank God for wanting
a relationship with us and me.

I appreciate those who helped me get this book ready for
publishing. Thanks to Joe DiCostanzo, Cass Daly, Art Chartier,
and especially my wife, Karen, who also encouraged me.

Special thanks to Covenant Books' staff who
were a big help and believed in this book.

INTRODUCTION

J ust as we want healthy relationships with others, God wants one with us too.

God initiated His relationship with us when He knew that we would be created. We can say that His relationship with us existed from this point in time. He has a purpose and a plan for our lives. He aims for you to be in a healthy spiritual relationship with Him. You are invited to willingly enter into this relationship. He wants a relationship with you. He loves you more than you will ever know or appreciate.

We are built to be relational. Yes, from the day we are born, human relationships begin. It is a family relationship that comes from a couple's relationship. We expect this relationship to be perfect in every way. As we grow up, we anticipate having friends and acquaintances in the neighborhood, school, work, and a variety of activities for which we participate to have fun or enjoy. We like to be loved and trusted. We want to love too, which means learning to trust in a person. Individuals want healthy relationships. But a healthy relationship is hard to come by.

Truth be said, we don't know how to have healthy relationships because of a variety of reasons:

First, we have baggage that blocks open communication and intimacy. Our expectations of people are so high that very few, if any, can fulfill. In the early stages of our lives and for a long time afterward, in addition to our extremely high expectations, our perception of reality can be false. We don't usually communicate our perceptions to others. This lack of communication leaves us with a wrong opinion of our relationship status. For example, one of our daughters thought that we didn't love her because the first time she talked back to us, we didn't get in her face as we had done with the other children. The truth was that we just thought she was having a bad day and out of character, so we ignored her misbehavior. It wasn't until she mentioned it that we could clarify the truth. But what if she hadn't? Her perception of us not loving her would have been wrong and maybe damaging to our relationship with her. Also, sometimes bad things happen to us, and it is hard to get past this hurt in our hearts to reconciling with the person who caused the harm. Our unrealistic expectations, false perceptions, and bad things hamper our abilities to have healthy relationships with God and others.

Second, we are broken, hurt, self-centered, and selfish people who find it hard to have perfectly healthy relationships. It is easy to get discouraged from working for good relationships and trusting others. We want instant healthy relationships, but it is a process and requires hard work and the grace of God.

Third, we live in a culture that encourages unhealthy relationships. Everyone wants to be happy. They expect others to make them happy, but it doesn't work that way. I cringe when a couple comes to see me for premarital counseling, and when I ask them, "Why do you want to get married?" their reply has sometimes been, "He or she makes me happy." I ask, "But what happens when he or she stops making you happy?" They might answer, "Then we will get divorced."

Last, our culture also encourages terrible relationship skills with the invention of social media. It provides us with the ability to vent our anger to people we don't know personally and probably will never know. Once after watching a show on evolution, I made a comment on Twitter about how the show didn't do a very excellent job of explaining the theory of evolution. Within seconds of this post, I got a tweet back and emails from the same person telling me how stupid I was for not believing in evolution. He assumed I didn't believe in evolution. He never asked me if I did or didn't. A relationship with this person seems impossible because he appeared to want to put me down beneath him. Social media encourages us to talk *about* people and not *to* people. We must do the opposite if we can ever think about having a healthy relationship.

God's love, truth, patience, honesty, forgiveness, goodness, mercy, faithfulness, power, and grace are greater than all the obstacles with which we were born, the culture provides, and the environment in which we are placed. The good news is that God can rescue us from all the obstacles. God's character and qualities can overcome our desire to run from Him or to ignore Him and to seek Him falsely. He overcame our brokenness and wrong decisions through Jesus Christ's work for us on the cross.

Despite all the obstacles to having healthy relationships, God wants us to have a healthy relationship with Him and those with whom we come into contact. And he provides a way for both. They both take time.

This book is about looking into a sample of biblical stories to see what they have to say about how God had a healthy relationship with some of the biblical characters and a nation. These stories also reveal how He envisions us to have a healthy relationship with Him and others. The variety of personalities and relationships makes scripture come alive and powerful. I hope that this book will lead you to have a more mature relationship with God and others.

1

The Relational Ball Gets Thrown
CREATION OF ADAM AND EVE (GENESIS 1–2)

Scripture tells us God created the heavens and the earth and all that is in it. He created the earth so there would be living creatures in the air, seas, and land. There are so many physical conditions in creation that are perfect for life to happen. For example, if the position of the axis of the earth was different by some tiny amount, then the earth would be consumed by the heat of the sun. Another example is the right amount of oxygen here for life—not too much and not too little.

In the first creation story, He created man and woman in His image. Yes, we are made to have the capacity to have similar character traits as God. We can be wise, loving, thinking, able to listen, kind, and compassionate. These are some examples of how we are like God, but we must not ever forget that we are different from God. We are not all knowing, present everywhere at the same time, and in total control of our lives. We are not God and will never be a god. We will always be distinctly different from God on earth and heaven.

Life is a gift from God. We didn't do anything to earn this precious gift.

God trusted humankind to be the steward of what He created on earth and maybe even in all of space. What an honor and distinction He gave to humanity. This responsibility was a pure gift because humankind hadn't done one single thing to earn this honor. Given this responsibility means humankind is superior to all other creatures. There is a great responsibility that comes with being a steward. Humankind is to preserve and protect all creation in a kind and orderly way. Adam was given the responsibility to name all the creatures.

In the second creation story, God created man; and from man's rib bone, He made woman. None of the other creatures, not one of them, was fit to be an adequate helper for man. Not even a loving dog or cat was suitable to be man's helpmate. It is clear from these stories that God didn't want humankind to be alone. He needed someone who was fit to be in a relationship with him so that other humans could be propagated to begin the relational chain of spouse, family, tribe, and nation. In these relationships, we can eventually learn the critical key to healthy relationships, which is the kind of love God has for us.

I believe this is clear from our stories about creation and Adam and Eve that humankind was created to be in a special relationship with God. This relationship was much different from all the other creatures. It was God's initiative that began the relationship. It was His idea, and it pleased Him because He said, "It was very good," after His creation of Adam and Eve was completed.

A question to ponder: God was very pleased with His creation of humans. Scripture tells us that He planned us before we were born. How does that make you feel?

2

The Wars Begins
REBELLION OF ADAM AND EVE (GENESIS 3)

Adam and Eve were in the garden where they had healthy food and spent time walking and talking with God. He did give them a soul or a will to choose who they would trust, respect, enjoy, worship, and obey. God gave Adam only one boundary: "You can eat from any tree in the garden except the tree of the knowledge of good and evil, for if you do, you will die." In other words, it would be the end of this special, intimate, spiritual relationship with humankind for now. It doesn't mean they would physically die right away. So this was a very loving act by God to warn them. God loved them and wanted them to live eternally with Him in paradise.

A serpent came along one day and spoke to Eve. A snake was the most cunning of all the wild animals. His message was a different voice than God's. The serpent's strategy was to put doubt into Eve's head and turn her allegiances from God to him. He questioned her about what God said. "Did you hear, right? Did God really mean what he said?" Then the real kicker was the serpent told her that she would be like God by knowing good and evil. (*Please stop, Eve! You are already like God—you are made in His image. You only know good now. This is enough to be in a relationship with the good God.*) But she didn't stop to think it over; she looked at the delightful fruit and wanted it so that she would have even greater wisdom. Then she ate from the tree, even though she had been told by Adam not to do so. She gave some of this delightful food to Adam to eat. He didn't object, even though he too knew better. They rejected God's gift of a relationship on His terms.

Their eyes were open to knowing that they had disobeyed God's words, and they felt shame for the first time. They covered themselves with fig tree leaves to cover their nakedness or their shame of rebellion. Their rebellion was the first shot fired at the enemy who was now God. They turned from listening to God to listening to a voice that opposed God. They valued the created over the Creator. At this point, there was no turning back.

In the evening, they heard God walking in the garden. Soon He would catch up with them and see that their shame and nakedness needed to be covered. They hid from Him. God knew perfectly well what happened because He is all knowing and called out to them, "Where are you?"

Adam was honest with God. He said that he heard God walking in the garden and was afraid because he was ashamed of being naked, so he hid. Of course, he should have been frightened. Adam just rebelled against God who loved him and provided His very best for both of them. (*We need to get ready to learn the consequences of their rebellion against God.*)

God knew Adam and Eve disobeyed Him and ate from the tree of knowledge of good and evil; and this is why they knew they were naked, covered themselves, and hid from Him. But He wanted Adam to continue being honest with Him. God asked, "Who told you that you were naked? Did you eat from the tree that I commanded you not to eat from?"

(*Adam, stop and think before you speak! Don't start the blame game! You are not going to, are you?*)

Adam blames God and then his wife Eve: "Well, I wouldn't have eaten the fruit if you hadn't given me Eve because she forced me to eat it. I had no choice. Don't blame me." God knows he is lying. (*Cover-ups can sometimes be worse than the crime.*)

The lies continue. God asks Eve, "What have you done?"

She replied, "Don't blame me. The serpent you created tricked me. I was outwitted. It wasn't my fault. I am a poor victim."

God doesn't have to hear anymore. They were guilty, and He was not. They broke the relationship, and God did not. He begins laying out the consequences. God could not be in their sinful presence, so He had them removed from the garden. First, God speaks to the serpent, who represents Satan, that he will be cursed more than any other animal. The serpent will now have to move by slithering on the ground without legs. Dust will always be in his face. (*Scientists recently found fossils of snakes with legs.*)

In addition to the spiritual war between humankind and God, which was caused by worshiping the created, there is a constant spiritual war between Satan and humanity. The conflict between Satan and humankind is caused by the lies and doubts Satan puts in our heads so we won't believe or reduce our faith in God.

Now God begins to reveal His plan to restore humanity to Himself and defeat Satan from having any more spiritual effects on people. He goes on to say that one of Eve's offspring will defeat Satan as revealed in the Book of Revelation when we are told that Satan will be sent to hell and remain there forever, along with his army of unbelievers. To reveal His plan, God tells Adam and us that Satan will strike the heal of this descendant by having him suffer terribly. We know that Jesus is the one who is spoken of here. In the movie *The Passion of the Christ*, the opening scene is Jesus praying to his Father at Gethsemane before his lonely journey of being arrested and crucified. With his face to the ground, a snake slithers right up to him. Jesus calmly stands up and crushes the head of the snake. This scene is a very potent image because God promised it would happen someday. The suffering offspring and the defeat of Satan are part of the plan to end the wars between God and humankind and Satan and humankind. God actively pursued His plan because of His love for all of his human creatures.

The woman was told that she would have more pain in child-birth and there would be a battle of self-wills between husbands and wives. After having listened to the voice of Satan, the relationship between husband and wife will become more complicated without following God's words.

Finally, Adam heard his fate. For them to eat, the land outside the garden, from which they were removed, has thorns and thistles, which will have to be removed by hard work and sweat. There will be only plants in this land to eat.

They will die and be returned to the dust of the ground from which they were created. Adam and Eve's new experience of suffering and grieving would begin.

God did not like the fig leaves that they used to cover them-selves, so he killed an animal. In His mercy, from this dead animal, He made coverings from the animal skins. In the Bible, *being clothed* often refers to the cover of God's righteousness or forgiveness and purity. We learn later that acts of disobedience to God will require the blood of a living creature to satisfy what was needed for reconcil-iation between God and humanity. Adam and Eve were forgiven, but that doesn't mean that there weren't consequences for their actions. They are accountable for their choices. Later, animal sacrifices were made to cleanse the sins of the Israelites so the relationship between God and them could continue in an imperfect way.

The relationship between husband and wife will now be problematic because of the introduction of the blame game and the war of wills. I know sometimes my ego and pride get in the way, and my first instinct is to blame my wife for the error or wrong decision in a meeting at church so I don't look bad. I get the "look" and know I messed up and need to repent for my blaming statement.

The relationship between God and all of humanity would be harmed and not be as intimate as planned for a long time. In the meantime, God will have relationships with individuals, tribes, and nations. He did so as part of His extensive plan to restore His relationship with all of humanity permanently. It would take one of Eve's offspring (Jesus) to restore this eternal relationship. The relationship between husband and wife would be improved and restored closer to what God meant for it to be by Eve's offspring too.

Adam and Eve went from a perfect life that listened to God to a life that questioned and rebelled against God. This rebellion led humankind from listening to God to shutting out His truths from our hearts. We either trust God or we trust part of His creation. The Bible stories explain that this fickleness is the new normal for humans after being removed from the garden. The consequences of this new normal resulted in humankind experiencing suffering. We began to experience pain—physical, emotional, mental, and spiritual. Another result seems to be that it is part of our nature to have a greater desire for something forbidden by God or humankind.

God has a marvelous plan for humanity when it comes to relationships and what a healthy relationship will be. He shows grace, mercy, kindness, and self-control as he executes His plan. We will begin to look at His plan for relationship restoration in His story of relationships with individuals, families, tribes, and nations.

A question to ponder: What is the worst thing you did to rebel against God and how does it feel, even with consequences, that you are totally forgiven and your relationship with God has been restored?

3

Listening Gains Knowledge
NOAH (GENESIS 6–9)

For a relationship to grow in the knowledge of one another, it is vital and critical to listen to the other. Without knowledge of the other, we cannot decide if we want a relationship with the person.

God knew Noah. He called him a righteous man who walked with Him. Noah spent time with the Lord every day and listened to Him. He got to know God better as he lived every day by trusting Him. (*We will learn that he will trust God in a big way.*)

One day, God spoke to Noah so he could get to know Him better by knowing His will: "I have determined to make an end of all flesh for the earth is filled with violence. Behold, I will destroy all of them. [*What?*] Make yourself an ark of gopher wood. Make rooms in the ark and cover it inside and out with pith.

"Here are the directions on how you are to make it: the length of the ark 450 feet, its breadth 75 feet, and its height 45 feet. Make a roof and finish it with a 1.5-foot top and set the door of the side of the ark. Make it with lower, second, and third decks. For behold, I will bring a flood of waters upon the earth to destroy all flesh.

Everything that is on the earth shall die. But I will establish my covenant with you, and you shall come into the ark—you, your sons, your wife, and your sons' wives—will join you.

"And of every living thing with flesh, you shall bring two of every sort into the ark to keep them alive with you. They shall be male and female. All the birds according to their kinds, the animals according to their kinds, every creeping thing of the ground according to its kind, and two of every sort shall come in the ark and keep them alive. Also, take with you every sort of food that is eaten and store it up. It shall serve as food for you and them."

Noah did this; he did all that God commanded him. (*Noah had to have known God before this instruction. It would have been an impossible task and responsibility for most people. What did Noah learn about God as he listened?*)

God is holy and pure, and He hates sin and evil. God was totally in control of His creation. He is wise and had a thought-out plan. Noah and his family were part of God's plan. God loved all of His creation and all the various kinds of birds and animals. He had provided food for them to take. God obviously wanted a relationship with Noah and his family beyond the flood. He was also committed to a two-way connection with every human. Listening to God resulted in more than knowing about God but knowing Him.

Then the Lord spoke and Noah listened, "Go to the ark, you and all your household. In seven days, I will send rain for forty days and forty nights, and every living thing I have made will die except all on my ark." Noah did what he commanded.

Just as God had said, it rained for forty days and nights, and the whole earth was covered. The ark started rising, and the water on the planet rose. Water also covered the mountains.

After a while, God had a high wind blow over the earth, and the water subsided. In seven months on the seventh day, the ark rested on the mountain of Ararat.

Noah sent a dove, but there was no place for it to land, so it returned. In seven days, he sent the dove again; in the evening, the dove returned with a fresh olive leaf. The dove was sent out a third time, and it didn't return to the ark. Noah removed the covering of the ark and saw that the water had subsided over the earth. A month later, God spoke to Noah and told him to leave the ark with his family and all the animals and birds. They were to scatter and populate the earth as a new beginning. Noah and God had a healthy relationship because they both knew each other well.

When we meet people, we know very little about them. As we spend time with them, we get to know who they really are. As people are willing to risk speaking about what they think and feel, the more we get to see the depth of the person. God and Noah had this kind of relationship. God talked, and Noah listened. Noah got to a point where he could trust his life and his family's to the Lord. God saved them, the animals, and the earth.

God had a difficult decision at this time because He hated any person who had broken his or her relationship with Him by loving the created things above the Creator. At the same time, He wanted to continue having a connection with all humans made in His likeness. Noah and the Ark were His answer to start over with humankind and still maintain His integrity.

A question to ponder: Noah listened to God. What is it like to have someone listen to you and they hear you?

4

Promise Maker and Keeper
ABRAM/ABRAHAM (GENESIS 12–25)

Abram's father and his pagan family moved to Haran. After his father died, the Lord spoke to Abram. God told Abram to leave Haran and all of his birth family behind. He would go to the land that God will show him, and there, his offspring will become a great nation. Abram will be blessed, and his name shall be great. It states that through him, all the families of the earth shall be blessed. These were the first of God's promises.

Abram was selected by God to be a great leader and whose faith would impact every family on the earth. God initiated this relationship by making promises that meant Abram was leaving his comfort zone and trusting God to fulfill His promises. Many relationships today are built on promises said out loud like our marriage vows or a parent's unspoken pledges to protect, train up, and love their children. Unfortunately, we don't or can't keep our promises perfectly as God does. Healthy relationships need promises to be made and kept.

At age seventy-five, Abram packs up all the possessions; and he, his wife Sarai, and his nephew Lot went as the Lord had told him. He had great faith and took God at His word. In a few days, they arrived at Canaan and then continued to Shechem. One problem was the Canaanites still lived in this land. There he built an altar to the Lord after God told him that He would give Abram this land for his children. This promise was his second promise. This act of building the first altar in this land was how Abram showed his thankfulness to the true God.

He kept moving around in this land and finally settled in Negeb. A severe famine struck the country, and he was forced to go to Egypt to survive. Egypt was a rich and powerful land. Being forced to go to Egypt would not be the last time Abram's people would end up going to Egypt for protection.

We will learn that Abram was a faithful man but not a perfect man and husband. The coward asked his wife to pretend she was his sister because she was beautiful and he would be killed if they knew that he was her husband. He pretended to be her brother so that his life would be spared and blessed. The problem was this meant she could be taken as someone's wife, and sure enough, no other than the man who ruled over Egypt wanted her as one of his wives. In exchange, the pharaoh gave Abram many animals like sheep, oxen, and donkeys.

God, being who He is, protected Sarai and inflicted great plagues on Egypt to prevent this lie from going any further. By the grace of God, pharaoh figures out the reason for a god to be mad at him and goes to Abram, upset—to put it mildly, to confront him about his lie. He immediately kicked the two of them out of Egypt. (*Thank you, God, for protecting Sarai because of Abram's fear.*) After all, this unfaithful event was not part of God's plan for Abram and Sarai and all the families of the earth.

Abram returned to Canaan. The Lord said to Abram after Lot had separated from him by going to Sodom, "Lift your eyes, and I will give you all the land that you can see in all directions. I give to you and your offspring, who will be greater in number than all the dust particles of the earth, all this land. Arise and go walk the length and breadth of this land." God repeated his former promise. Again he was so thankful for God's promise that he built an altar in Hebron where he had moved his tent.

There was a war that took place among various kings. After Abram and the kings who were with him returned after capturing Chedorlaomer, a king named Melchizedek came out to greet Abram and brought bread and wine to celebrate the victory. This is a precursor to the Christian celebration of communion. He blessed Abram by saying, "Blessed be Abram by God Most High, Possessor of heaven and earth; and blessed be God Most High, who has delivered your enemies into your hand." (*Others noticed the relationship Abram had with the one true God.*)

In a vision, the Lord said, "Fear not, Abram. I am your shield; your reward will be great."

But Abram replied, "I am still childless, and my heir is Eliezer in my household."

God corrected his thinking, "No, your heir will be your very own son!"

He took him outside his tent and said, "Look toward heaven and number the stars, if you are able to count them, and this will be the number of offspring you will have."

Abram believed the Lord, despite many years of childlessness. The Lord considered Abram righteous because of his faith and not for any of his works. As we will learn later, trust is key to a relationship with God.

Abram wanted to know for sure he was going to possess the land as promised. The Lord told him to cut a heifer, a female goat, and a ram—all three years old—as well as a turtledove and a pigeon. The birds were not cut in half. This killing sounds very strange to us, but this was a common practice in these times when a covenant was made between two parties. Both parties walked between the pieces of animals to seal the agreement. It was like a contract today. If one of the parties broke it, then he also would be cut in half to pay the price for breaking it. (*That would be a motivation to keep your word.*)

Abram fell into a deep sleep, and a great darkness came upon him. Then the Lord made another promise, which would be kept. He told him that their offspring would be servants in a foreign land for four hundred years. He will bring judgment on this land and rescue them from it. They would get God's Promised Land later. God told Abram he would live to old age. To end the dream, the Lord revealed His presence by the representation of a fire pot and a flaming torch. The agreement was completed by His presence between the cut animals. Only God was there between the pieces. The Lord repeated His promise that Abram's offspring would be given the land.

This soap opera doesn't settle down any time soon. Sarai had not borne an heir, so she suggested to Abram to take her Egyptian servant to produce a child. He listened to his wife's advice, and then she gave Hagar to Abram to be a second wife. (*Three is a crowd. It was then and still is today.*)

Hagar got pregnant, and she acted haughty around Sarai. This behavior didn't sit well with Sarai, and she blamed it on Abram. The blame game continues. He responded, "She is your servant, and you have the power to do what you want." She then began treating Hagar harshly.

The Lord addressed Hagar at a well and told her that this wasn't her fault and that a son would be born to her; and he would be a great leader, and from him, great multitudes would result. A son was born by Abram, and his name was Ishmael.

The Lord appeared to Abram once again. He wanted to make another covenant between Abram and Himself. Remember, the last agreement was made just by God. This time, Abram was invited to join God in the transaction. The Lord desired for Abram to be blameless; He wanted Abram to stop doing foolish things that hurt their relationship. Abram's name was changed to Abraham, which means "the father of a multitude of nations." Kings will come from these nations.

This promised covenant was not only between God and Abraham but included his descendants after him and was an ever-lasting covenant agreement. This covenant was the beginning of the relationship between God and the nation of Israel. It was one of the nations promised and became the chosen nation for God. He again promised the land of Canaan and stated, "I will be their [the nation of Israel's] God."

God gave them a sign and seal of the covenant, which was the requirement that all men in Abraham's household be circumcised and all the male children afterward on the eighth day after birth. It was meant to be a reminder to the men of this agreement between Abraham and God and their participation in this everlasting cove-nant. This agreement was how the nation of Israel was formed.

God kept the relationship going by reaffirming His promise of a son. He told him that he and Sarai would have a son and she would be blessed and from her will come nations and kings. He was to call his wife Sarah.

Abraham fell on his face, laughed, and said to himself, "Shall a child be born to a man who is very old? You must mean Ishmael."

God responded, "No, your wife Sarah will bear you a son in a year from now, and you shall call him Isaac. I will keep my covenant agreement with him and his offspring." Then God went up from Abraham.

Abraham then has all the men in his household circumcised, including Ishmael. This act shows his willingness to participate in the covenant and relationship with God.

Abraham journeyed to Negeb to live where Abimelech was king. (*He didn't learn the lesson of trusting his life to the Lord.*) Again He lied and told the king that Sarah was his sister. The king sent for Sarah and took her to be another wife. God intervened—this time, through a dream that made it very clear that if Abimelech touched Sarah, he would die. The king defended himself by insisting that he was innocent of this sin because Abraham and Sarah lied about their relationship. God agreed and went on to tell him that Abraham, a prophet, would pray for the king.

The king was furious and called Abraham into his presence, "What have you done to us?"

Abraham defended himself, "I thought this place had no fear of God and you all would kill me. She is indeed sort of my sister. She is the daughter of my father but not my mother. So I asked her to protect me by telling everyone that she was my sister so I would not be killed."

Abimelech gave him land, servants, and animals. Abraham prayed to God; and He healed Abimelech, his wife, and the female slaves so they could bear children.

The Lord visited Sarah, and He did what He had promised. A son was born to her, and he was named Isaac. Again, God kept His promise.

Now for one of the most significant and dramatic stories of Abraham's and God's relationship, God told Abraham, "Take your son, Isaac, whom you love immensely, to the land of Moriah and offer him there as a burnt offering on one of the mountains of which I shall tell you." (*What kind of request is this of any father? How did Abraham react to this request?*)

He rose early in the morning and packed up his donkey and brought along with him two young men as well as Isaac. He cut the wood to be used for the horrible sacrifice of burned flesh. After three days, he saw the place from afar to where he was supposed to make the request.

He said to the two young men that he and Isaac would go over there to worship God the Father and then return to them. Abraham so trusted God that he knew God would provide somehow. He placed the wood for the offering on Isaac, and he took the fire and knife. Later, Isaac asked the gut-wrenching question, "Father, where is the lamb for the burnt offering?"

Abraham then said, "God himself will provide the lamb for a burnt offering, my son!"

They continued until they reached the place where God had told Abraham. He built the altar, laid the wood on top, and bound Isaac. His precious son was put on top of the wood on the altar. He did the unthinkable. He reached out his hand with the knife to kill his God-promised son. (*If this were a movie, the tenseness and volume of the music would have the audience in great pain and stress.*)

From heaven, an angel of Lord for God called out to Abraham, "Abraham, Abraham."

28

He responded, "Here I am."

And then God said, "Do not lay your hand on the boy or do anything to him. For now, I know you trust Me, seeing that you have not withheld your son, your only son, from Me."

Abraham looked up and saw a ram caught in a thicket by its horns. Abraham went and got it and sacrificed it to God instead of his only son. Abraham named the place "God will provide."

The angel of the Lord called from heaven a second time, "Because you were willing to obey my request, I will indeed bless you and multiply your offspring in the numbers of the stars in heaven and the sand on the seashore. Your family will have the land I promised, and all the nations of the earth will be blessed."

Abraham's relationship with God had matured. He not only trusted God with his own life but with the life of his only son. He didn't seem to doubt for a second God would keep His promises, which meant He would not have to kill Isaac. He truly believed God would provide the lamb for the sacrifice. God did. Abraham is known as the father of faith. This kind of faith impacted families all over the earth, even to this day.

God gave Abraham and Sarah a son, their offspring who created the nation of Israel and was given the Promised Land of Canaan, even though it was taken from other inhabitants. This son, Isaac, was part of God's plan; and we will see His plan unfold as the many relational stories are revealed in this book.

God was all in to have a relationship with Abraham and Israel as well as all the families of the earth. He made promises and kept all of them. Promises kept always strengthens trust in relationships. God showed He could be trusted. He initiated the relationship and protected the two of them when they made a mess of things.

Questions to ponder: God started the relationship with Abram and Sarai. He made them promises. Do you remember a promise that you made and didn't keep? What would you have done differently? Why?

5

Grace in the Thick of Brokenness
Joseph (Genesis 35–50)

Every family has its conflicts. All families don't function in healthy ways all the time. There is jealousy, fear, hatred, uncertainty, pride, competitiveness, addiction, and unforgiveness, to name a few things, that create brokenness and separation in a family. Joseph's family was no exception to dysfunction.

It started way before Joseph was born. Jacob, his father, was the younger of twin children to Isaac. Jacob and his mother, Rebekah, who loved him more than his brother, plotted against his twin brother, Esau. Being the oldest, Esau was entitled to a special blessing from Isaac, who was near death. Jacob and his mom planned to trick the already-blind Isaac to give the blessing to Jacob instead. Esau came home to receive the blessing, and Isaac said that he had already given it to Jacob, who had deceived him. Esau was furious because Jacob had tricked him out of his birthright inheritance earlier and now the special blessing. The name *Jacob* meant "deceive/cheat." This rivalry leads to estrangement. Jacob fled in fear. Over time, by God's love and grace (gift unmerited and undeserved), these two brothers reconciled.

Jacob, who was renamed by God to be *Israel* (which means "he strives with God or God fighter"), had two wives. With Leah, whom he was tricked into marrying, had six children of which Reuben was the oldest. Rachel, his favorite wife, bore two children, Joseph and Benjamin. With Rachel's servant, he had two more; and finally, with Leah's servant, he had another two, totaling twelve. (*This story is quite a soap opera but hard to think someone would have the imagination to think something like this up. Here is the reality of the family's brokenness.*)

It is not surprising that Joseph was Jacob/Israel's favorite. (*Having a favorite child is not a good idea and always leads to brokenness.*) If anyone should have known this, it was Jacob. (*But many times, we end up doing what we know and are familiar, instead of what is right.*) Jacob gave Joseph a coat of many colors, which marks the son to be the next leader of the family, leaving out the oldest son, Reuben. This favoritism was so apparent to the other boys.

One morning Joseph told his brothers about a dream he had: "We were binding sheaves in the field, and my sheaf stood upright. And your sheaves gathered and bowed down to mine." The brothers interpreted the dream to mean that he was to rule and reign over them. Their hatred for Joseph grew even stronger.

Well, Joseph had another dream, which included his parents as well as his brothers. When he told it to all of them, Jacob rebuked him for having such a foolish dream that meant they would all bow before Joseph. (*Joseph was young, or should he have known better?*)

The brothers were tending to Jacob's flock of sheep in Shechem. Jacob asked Joseph to go and find them and report back how they and the flock were doing. Joseph obediently packed up, and off he went to check up on his brothers, a task he favored.

They saw him coming far off on a hill wearing his multicolored coat. Joseph had no idea that their hatred for him had grown to such a crescendo and what was coming his way. They quickly conspired to kill him. Reuben objected to killing him; instead, they put him in a pit with no water. (*Wouldn't he die if he were kept there?*) As they were about to have lunch, they looked up and saw a group of foreigners coming with their goods to sell in Egypt. (*Egypt seems to be a thread in many of the biblical stories.*) Judah suggested that they sell him for twenty shekels of silver. Off Joseph went to Egypt. There was no indication that Joseph fought them; yes, he was outnumbered by his older brothers.

Well, the brothers had to lie to their father why Joseph was gone. They told their father that Joseph was killed by a wild beast and gave him the coat of many colors covered with lamb's blood. Jacob went into grieving that rocked his soul. The sons and daughters tried to comfort him. (*They might have used words that probably were not so helpful like "He is heaven now or a better place." One must go through their grieving in their way and in their own time.*) Jacob wept a lot for Joseph because he loved him so much.

Meanwhile, Joseph was sold to Potiphar, the captain of the guard of the pharaoh. The Lord was with him, and he became very successful. Potiphar noticed the gift of success Joseph had received from God. He put Joseph in charge of his house and everything that he owned. For Joseph's sake, God blessed his master's house and field. Potiphar trusted him entirely and worried about nothing but what he ate to fill his belly.

Not only did Potiphar like Joseph, but his wife liked the build and looks of the handsome young Joseph. She had eyes for him and took action by asking him to lie with her. Joseph said, "No, your husband has given me access to everything he owns but you. How can I do this wickedness and sin against God?"

He left her immediately, but this didn't stop her by inviting him again day after day. One day when he was in the house tending to his work, the house was vacant except for the two of them. She grabbed his garment and invited him once again. He ran out of the house with the garment still in her hand.

She called the men of the household and told them that the Hebrew was there to laugh at them, saying, "He came into my room, wanting to lie with me like I was a piece of property. I screamed in a loud voice." As proof, he left his garment here. She put the garment on the floor next to her until the master arrives at the bedroom later that day. She told him that Joseph tried to rape her and showed him Joseph's garment that she had pulled off him. The master became furious and had Joseph put in prison for this untrue heinous act against his wife. By God's grace, he was still alive. No trial, just her word for it. (*What happened in prison should not surprise us.*)

The Lord was with Joseph and showed his steadfast love by having the keeper (warden) of the prison favor Joseph. He was put in charge of all the other prisoners. The Lord made Joseph succeed. (*I wonder if the Lord made us succeed in our careers when He needed us to do so?*)

The cupbearer and baker of the pharaoh committed offenses that angered him. They were given to the captain of the guard to watch in prison where Joseph was. By the grace of God, Joseph was assigned to them and attended to them.

One night, both the cupbearer and baker each had a personal dream. The next morning, Joseph saw they were upset and asked them why. They replied, "We each had a dream and no one to interpret them for us." Joseph said that interpretation belongs to God, and he asked them to tell their dreams to him.

The cupbearer went first. His dream was this: "There was a vine before me, and on the vine were three branches. As soon as it budded, its blossoms opened up, and the clusters ripened into grapes. Pharaoh's cup was in my hand, and I took the grapes and pressed them into Pharaoh's cup and placed the cup in Pharaoh's hand."

Joseph gave him this interpretation: "The three branches are three days. In this time, Pharaoh will pardon you and restore you to your old office. Then he asked the cupbearer to remember him to Pharaoh so he could be freed from this place because he was innocent."

When the baker heard that the cupbearer's interpretation was favorable, he told his dream to Joseph: "There are three cake baskets full of baked goods for the pharaoh, but the birds are eating the goods from the basket on my head."

Joseph told him what this meant: "The three cake baskets are three days. In three days, the pharaoh will release you but will hang you. The birds will eat your flesh as you hang."

It was the pharaoh's birthday, and he did precisely to them as Joseph had described their dreams. However, the cupbearer forgot about Joseph and his God-given gift to interpret dreams correctly.

After two whole years, Pharaoh dreamed that he was standing by the Nile, and there came out of the river seven cows, attractive and plump, and they fed in the reed grass. Seven other cows, ugly and thin, came up out of the Nile after them and stood by the other cows on the bank of the Nile. And the ugly thin cows ate up the seven nicer-looking ones. Then Pharaoh awoke. He fell back asleep and dreamed a second dream. Seven ears of grain, plump and good, were growing on a stalk. Also, seven ears were thin and blighted by the east wind grew on the stalk. The thin ones ate the plump ones. He was very troubled by these dreams and called all the magicians and wise men of the land. But not one could interpret these dreams.

The cupbearer finally remembered Joseph's gift of dream interpretation. He told Pharaoh. Joseph was brought to interpret the dreams. Joseph said, "By the grace of God and not me, Pharaoh will receive a favorable answer." Joseph eagerly listened as Pharaoh told of his dreams.

Joseph then gave the interpretation that God gave him: "Both the seven cows and seven ears are seven years. The weaker cows and ears mean that there will be a very severe famine for the seven years. This famine will follow seven years of great plenty."

He recommended to the pharaoh that he appoint a wise man and give him the authority over the land. A fifth of the produce in each of the seven years of plenty needs to be stored away so that Egypt will have food during the seven years of the severe famine.

Pharaoh asked the servants, "Is there someone in our land that has the Spirit of God in him?" Then Pharaoh appointed Joseph because he was so wise and discerning. Joseph was given great power and appointed second in command of all of Egypt.

Joseph was willing to serve the pharaoh. He carried out his recommendations. He gathered in reserve so much food, it couldn't be counted. This reserve prepared them for the famine. Joseph opened up the storehouses and sold the produce to the Egyptians. The famine was so severe people from all the lands around Egypt came to buy food to survive.

Jacob and the Hebrews in Canaan were no exception. Joseph's brothers, except Benjamin, were sent to Egypt to buy produce. (*This excursion was not a coincidence but a "God-incidence."*)

His brothers arrived in Egypt. They immediately went to the man who was selling the food. They bowed, just as Joseph's childhood dream showed, with their faces to the ground. He recognized his brothers, but they did not recognize him. He spoke roughly to them. With a raised voice, he asked, "Where are you from?"

They told him, "Canaan."

Joseph yelled, "You are spies and have come to see our weakness."

They replied emphatically as protection, "No, my lord, your servants have come to buy food. We are the sons of one man. We are honest. Your servants have never been spies."

He repeated his statement about being spies. They said, "We are twelve brothers, but the youngest one is not here, and one is dead."

Joseph put them in custody for three days and had a plan to see his younger brother in Egypt. On the third day, he took Simeon from them and bound him in front of their eyes. He told them, "Take a little grain for your families and return with the youngest son so that you will not die."

Before Joseph seized Simeon, they had spoken among themselves and didn't realize this powerful man in front of them was Joseph and could understand every word they said. All of them believed God was punishing them for what they had done to Joseph. His heart broke at these words, so he left the room and wept.

Without their knowledge, Joseph ordered grain to be put in each of their bags as well as the money they used to pay for the grain. He also provided provisions for the trip home.

At the first lodging place, one of them went to his bag on his donkey to feed them and found the money in the mouth of the pack. When the others were told, they freaked out. "What has God done to us?"

After his sons told Jacob what happened, they unpacked their bags and found money in all their bags as well. All became afraid. Jacob was distraught at what was going on and refused to let them return, believing Simeon was already dead. He said to them, "Benjamin is the only one left." (*Ouch, Dad.*)

Reuben, who loved to be the savior, said, "Let me take Benjamin back, and I promise to return with him. If I don't, you can kill my two sons."

Jacob responded, "If Benjamin is harmed, this will kill me."

The famine got very bad, and Jacob's family had to have more food to survive. He told his sons to go back to Egypt and buy more food. The boys said that they would not go unless Benjamin accompanied them because the leader promised to kill them. Jacob/Israel became mad for telling the leader about Benjamin.

They replied, "He inquired into our family thoroughly until we had to tell him there were two more brothers, the youngest and one who had died."

Judah also promised to bring Benjamin home safely, and if not, he would be to blame.

Jacob finally agreed, "You must take some gifts like pistachio nuts to this man and take double the money. Return the money you found in your bags and hope that it was an oversight."

Jacob prayed for them, "Almighty, grant Your mercy before this Egyptian man, and may he send back your brother left there and Benjamin." Jacob didn't believe that good was going to come from this adventure.

When they arrived in Egypt, they stood before Joseph. He saw Benjamin and was delighted. He told the steward to invite them to his house at noon for a feast.

But the brothers were afraid and didn't understand why they were to go to his house. They went anyway. They pulled the steward aside and explained the error with the money in their bags. The steward replied, "Peace to you, do not be afraid. Your God and the God of your father has put treasure in your sacks for you." In other words, God gave them, through Joseph, a gift that they didn't deserve. As they were about to be brought into Joseph's house, they were given water, had their feet washed, and given food for their donkeys.

They brought in their presents and again bowed before him. He first asked if their father was well and still alive. "Yes," they replied.

Joseph then played dumb. "Is this your youngest brother of whom you spoke? God be gracious to you, my son." It was too much for Joseph to see Benjamin; he went to his chamber and wept again.

He controlled himself and ordered the food to be served. The Egyptians ate together, and the brothers ate together. The Egyptians could not eat with them because it would have been an abomination if they had. After the law was given to Moses, this would be true of the Hebrews eating with the unclean Egyptians.

When the food was brought to the brothers, Benjamin received five times the amount as the others. They were amazed. They drank and were merry with Benjamin.

Now it was time for Joseph to get some more revenge on his brothers. He told the steward to return their money a second time and to put his gold and silver cups in Benjamin's sack. They left to return to Canaan, when the steward and his men approached them. "You have stolen the governor's gold and silver cups."

The brothers said, "Oh no, you have got it all wrong. There is no way. Remember, we returned the money from the first visit."

The steward demanded that their sacks be inspected. He began with the oldest, down to the youngest. It is in Benjamin's sack that he found the supposedly stolen goods. He arrested them all and returned them to Joseph.

When they arrived, he continued with this cruel game. "Benjamin must stay with me as my servant, and the rest of you return to your father."

They all freaked out big time.

Judah, remembering he promised to take the blame, eventually spoke up and tried to bargain with Joseph, "I will stay in Benjamin's place because it would kill our father if he didn't return. Our father loves him so much."

It was way too much for Joseph to hear. He ordered all the Egyptians to leave him, and he wept bitterly and so loudly that even the household of the pharaoh heard him. He returned and now became honest with them. "I am your brother Joseph." (*They couldn't believe their ears. They were in shock like a person whose precious wife died suddenly in a car crash.*)

Joseph went on by extending his grace on them, saying, "Don't be hard on yourselves for selling me. God went before us and had a plan to preserve the lives of our families. It was not you who sent me here—it was God. It was by His grace that your jealousy and hatred for me enabled our family to survive and to be reconciled so that we can be together once again. We can praise God for His gift."

They returned to Canaan and brought everyone back to Egypt. Jacob and Joseph were reunited. With the pharaoh's blessing, they settled in the place called Goshen. They lived in Egypt for four hundred years, just like God had told Abraham.

God had a plan and made an effort to use brokenness to bring the family and nation of Israel even stronger and faithful. Even though Joseph experienced hard times, God was always with him and helped him succeed at just the right time. He was a great witness to the people of Egypt. They knew God was with Joseph and was the one behind his success. God's plan resulted in saving Israel from the famine. The relationship with the nation of Israel and God continued.

God's grace had them overcome their deep-seated tensions over relationships in Jacob's family. Many members were guilty of causing some dysfunction and stress on family relationships. Grace was shown by Reuben and Judah at times to keep the peace. Jacob didn't seem to have a clue, though he did let them return, knowing the risk of losing Benjamin. Maybe it was forced grace. Joseph eventually extended grace to his brothers to ease their guilt and pain. Usually, someone has to step up first to extend grace when relationships are on the brink of disaster. Grace is essential to have healthy relationships when it is needed in difficult times.

Because God's grace is given to us, we can learn to extend grace to others. Yes, we can give a gift of—let's say—forgiveness to the other person to save the relationship. Grace is not enabling someone to continue bad behavior. It is a key ingredient in a healthy relationship because there will always be times of differences and hurt in a relationship. Grace unites and heals. Relationships are hard and require intentional effort. Grace is not a natural reaction for us but is worth the effort to give an undeserved gift to help solidify our relationships, just like God has solidified His relationship with us. God's grace saved the nation of Israel and prepared them for the next adventure of escaping from Egypt when they were abused and oppressed. They needed to return to the Promised Land.

We will learn God's grace saved us, who will be from every nation on this earth. It was part of God's plan to reconcile us to Him.

Questions to ponder: Has anyone ever given you an undeserved and unmerited gift that you couldn't pay back? How did you feel?

6

Patience Is Needed
Moses (Exodus 1–9)

Moses was called by God to be a leader of the Hebrews living in Egypt. God had to work hard until Moses trusted Him with His call to be a leader. God needed patience with Moses because he was hardheaded and weak. It had to be frustrating to God.

The Hebrew population grew in numbers, and the new pharaoh didn't know the history of Joseph. He was concerned that if a war broke out, the Hebrews would leave Egypt and join their enemies to fight against them. He had them build the cities of Pithom and Raamses, but they continued growing in number. And as they increased, so did Pharaoh's anxiety. He decided to make them slaves and work them very hard in construction and the fields. But they multiplied even more. Then he commanded all of his people that every male Hebrew child must be thrown into the Nile to drown to stop this massive growth.

Moses was born, and what was going to happen to him? His mother hid him for three months. Then he was placed in a basket that was protected in the reeds on the river. Pharaoh's daughter saw the basket and had it lifted to view it. Inside, she saw a baby Hebrew boy. She felt pity for the boy. The sister of Moses ran down to this woman and asked if she should get a Hebrew nurse to care for the child?

"Yes, and I will pay her for it," the Pharaoh's daughter said, and the baby's mother came to take care of him.

When the boy got older, she brought him back to Pharaoh's daughter to keep. She named him Moses, which means "I drew him out of the water."

When he became an adult, he observed how his people were being treated. He saw an Egyptian beating one of his kind. When he thought no one was looking, he took matters into his own hands by killing the violent Egyptian. At first, he didn't realize that he was seen doing this. When he found out the truth, he ran away to the land of Midian.

Conditions in Egypt became so bad that the Hebrews called out to God for help. And God heard their cries.

Moses was tending to the flock of his father-in-law, Jethro, and moved them to Horeb, the mountain of God. An angel of the Lord appeared in a fire in the middle of a bush, but it had not burnt up.

Moses turned to look at it when God spoke to him, "I have heard the cries of my people and seen the suffering they have experienced at the hands of the Egyptians. I will come down to free them. I have called you and will send you to Pharaoh to bring them out of Egypt back to the Promised Land."

Moses cried out, "What, who am I to go to Pharaoh to do this?" (*Moses had a false humility. He wanted to be excused from this call.*)

God said, "Relax, I will be with you. The sign that will convince you is when my people are out of Egypt, and then you shall serve me on this mountain." (*Notice how God reached out to connect with Moses. God called Moses, and this was more about God than Moses.*)

Moses, still not buying into his call, asked, "If my people ask me your name, what shall I say?"

"Tell them, I AM WHO I AM," God said. "Tell the people and the elders that the God of their fathers—Abraham, Isaac, and Jacob—had appeared to me and told me that He has seen what is being done to them and heard their cries. I will bring you out of this place to the land of milk and honey. They will listen to your voice. Then you and the elders will go to the king of Egypt and tell him that the Lord God has met with us and we want to go into the wilderness for three days to make a sacrifice to Him. I know he will not let you go, so I will do mighty wonders against him and his people, who will force him to let you go. You will go but not empty-handed."

Thinking—or, at least, hoping—God had asked the wrong person, Moses said, "They will not believe me or listen to me."

God tried patiently to build up Moses' confidence by having Moses do three things: The first was to take the staff in his hand and throw it to the ground, and it changed into a serpent. The next thing was to put his hand inside his cloak and then remove it. It became leprous, and then he was told to put it back and remove it. *Bam!* It was normal. And if these two weren't convincing, Moses was to take some water from the Nile and pour it on the ground to have it change to blood.

For most people, all this would have been more than enough. These weren't enough for Moses, exclaiming, "I have no experience in speaking. Besides that, I am slow at speech and tongue." (*Some think Moses stuttered.*)

Again the Lord patiently asked Moses, "Who has made man's mouth? Is it not I, the Lord? Therefore, go, and I will be with your mouth and teach you what to say."

Moses was so afraid, he didn't hear or believe God. Then he told God what was really on his heart: "Please send someone else." Moses knew he didn't have the skills, but God knew He could transform Moses.

The Lord began to lose his patience. (*Can you blame him?*) The Lord tells him, "Aaron can speak well, so the two of you will go. I will teach you both what to say and do. He shall speak for you to the people, and you shall be as God to him."

Moses asked his father-in-law, Jethro, if he could go back to Egypt to see if his brothers were still alive. Jethro said, "Go in peace," and off Moses went.

The Lord told Aaron to meet Moses on his way back. Moses told him everything the Lord said and did. The two of them went to the elders, and Aaron spoke to them. They believed the two of them and were overwhelmed that God had heard their prayers and seen their afflictions. They worshiped God with grateful hearts. Moses and Aaron especially did because it went as smooth as buttering toast with melted butter.

Somehow, Moses and Aaron got permission to speak to Pharaoh. They explained that their God had come to them and wanted them to have a festival and sacrifice to Him for three days.

The king of Egypt laughed and responded, "I don't know this God of yours, and why should I take them away from their important work for us?"

Aaron replied, "If we don't do this, then the God of Israel will bring pestilence and the sword upon you."

Vindictively, the king ordered that the Jews should no longer be given straw to make their bricks; they would have to gather it themselves without reducing the number of bricks they were required to complete each day.

When the people of Israel heard this bad news, they were ready to die.

Moses called out to God and asked, "Why have you done evil to our people? Why did you even send me? My speaking to Pharaoh in your name has done no good and only evil. Besides that, You have not delivered Your people at all."

God responded to Moses, "I have made myself known to Abraham, Isaac, and Jacob as God Almighty. I kept my covenant with them and gave them the land of Canaan. I have heard the groans of the people of Israel. I will not forget my covenant, and I will take them back to Canaan. You are my people, and I will be your God."

Moses and Aaron were next directed to tell the people, but they were so broken in spirit as they did not believe the two of them. Moses was very discouraged and even feeling hopeless. But God hadn't given up on Moses or His people.

God told them to go back to Pharaoh. He assured Moses, as His ambassador, that he would speak with authority and power. (*See how God was bringing Moses along.*) As his prophet, Aaron will deliver the message given to him by Moses.

God goes on to say to Moses and Aaron that the Egyptians will know He is the Lord when He does significant damage to the Egyptians before Pharaoh lets them leave to return to Canaan. The two of them ignored their negative feelings and obeyed the Lord.

The Lord tells them that when Pharaoh commands them to prove what they have told him, Aaron should throw down his staff and it will turn into a serpent. They did as God commanded. Then

Pharaoh told his magicians to match it. They did, but Aaron's staff ate up all the magician's serpents. Pharaoh's heart remained hardened.

God planned to drag out this whole situation by doing many plagues on Egypt. God began carrying out his plan to have Pharaoh let the Hebrews leave.

After the plague of the flies, Pharaoh called Moses and Aaron to come to him to agree that they may sacrifice to their God. It was at this time Moses found his voice. (*Some say that Moses stopped stuttering when he replied to the king of Egypt.*)

Moses said, "If we sacrifice an animal that is disgusting to your people, they will stone us. We must go on a three-day journey to sacrifice to our God as he told us."

Pharaoh countered by saying, "Okay, but don't go very far away. Plead to your God for me."

Moses went and prayed to the Lord, and God removed the flies from the Egyptian land. Pharaoh hardened his heart and did not let the Hebrews go. (*How much more will Pharaoh need to change his mind?*)

As God continued with the plagues, Egyptian livestock died, boils appeared on the people, hail rained down on them, locusts ate their grain, darkness fell, and the death of the firstborn afflicted the Egyptians and the Egyptian livestock. As these plagues progressed, Moses's leadership became stronger and more confident. The Egyptians realized the power of the Hebrew God and wanted them out of their country. God had gotten the Hebrews' attention, and they understood that Moses was God's man and that his purpose was to lead them out of Egypt and back to the land of milk and honey. Pharaoh let them go.

Before the final plague of the death of the firstborn that affected every household in Egypt, except the Hebrew ones, God introduced the practice of Passover. The Hebrew people were to take an unblemished lamb and put its blood on the doorpost of their homes so they would be protected from the killing of their firstborns. This memorial was significant in that it pointed to the blood of a perfect lamb in the future that also would save them, not just one time of being in slavery in Egypt but for all eternity. Jesus celebrated the Passover meal on Thursday before he was crucified on the cross and introduced at this meal a new covenant with God's people in all the nations of the earth.

Moses led the people out of Egypt safely, just as God had planned and promised. Pharaoh and his army chased the Hebrews. The Jews crossed the Red Sea safely when the water divided, and by the hand of God, the Egyptians were swallowed up and drowned by the returning water. (*Remember the promise God made to Abram about His nation being captive for four hundred years, and then He would bring judgment on the land and rescue them. This was the end of four hundred years.*)

In this story, we saw how God was patient with Moses and helped him along and grew him as the leader of the Hebrew people who had given up all hope in God and didn't trust Moses to be their leader. God knew Moses experienced what it was like to live under the control of others who had kept him in bondage from being who he was meant to be. He was to be a great leader to the Hebrew people whom God had chosen to be free. Moses's true self was hidden until God patiently revealed it to him.

In all relationships, patience is required because people change and circumstances change. These changes can put stress on the relationship, which can lead to impatience and put even more tension in the relationship. God's timetable isn't always ours, so we also need to learn and gain patience with God, knowing He is both good and He knows what He is doing all the time. God has patience with you too.

Questions to ponder: Did anyone ever show patience with you? What was it like? How did it affect your relationship with the person?

7

Trust Is All You Need
Joshua and the Battle of Jericho (Joshua 5–6)

A lot had happened since the last chapter on patience. Moses went on to be a great leader. God gave him the Ten Commandments for the people, which is the basis for our Western law. This is why you often see the Ten Commandments on the walls of our courts. The ark of the covenant was built and is famous in the *Indiana Jones* movies. It was a symbol of the presence of Israel's God with the people while in the wilderness for forty years after he got them out of bondage from the Egyptians. The ark was a portable box and contained the two stone tablets with the Ten Commandments, Aaron's rod that had produced fruit, and a golden urn holding some of the manna from the wilderness. At the time of this story, the priests were the ones to carry it.

The first generation that was circumcised did not make it to the Promised Land because of their rebellion against God, and this included Moses. Moses did make it to the spiritual Promised Land, as revealed in the transfiguration story in the Gospel books.

God called Joshua to replace Moses to lead the Hebrews into Canaan. Before the battle at Jericho, God told Joshua to circumcise all the men in his generation because they never had it done before! These circumcisions renewed the covenant relationship of the people with the living God. He had removed the burden that the Egyptians had put on them. He called the land where they stayed Gilgal, and it was in enemy territory.

The people kept the practice of the Passover to remind themselves of what God had done for them. He saved them from bondage and death. He didn't have to but wanted to because it was part of His plan to save all those who have faith in Him.

One day Joshua was standing on a cliff overlooking the City of Jericho. He turned around and saw a man standing in front of him with a sword drawn in his hand. He wanted to know who this was. It was believed to be an angel. When the man said that he was the commander of the Lord's army, Joshua fell on his face to worship him. He was told to take off his sandals because he was standing on holy ground. This same thing was said to Moses when he saw a bush burning that didn't get destroyed.

Jericho was locked up tighter than a wooden drum for wine. No one went in, and no one left. The people of Jericho were scared to death of the Hebrew people because they had heard what the Hebrew God had done in Egypt and the promise made to them to have their land. (*The Egyptians must have spread the word.*)

The Lord gave Joshua bizarre instructions on how to proceed into battle against Jericho. (*Generals Eisenhower, MacArthur, Schwarzkopf, and Powell would have thought they would be crazy to follow these orders. Let's see if God knew what He was doing.*)

Some priests carried the ark of the covenant, and alongside them, seven priests with seven rams' horns blew them continually. The armed men walked before them, and the rear guard followed the priests. Behind them, the people walked around Jericho one time for six days. On the seventh day, they marched around the city seven times. Then Joshua told all the people this, "Shout, for the Lord has given you the city. And the city and all that is within it shall be devoted to the Lord for destruction. But you are to keep yourselves from the things devoted to destruction. Don't take any of these things or you will put all of us in the path of destruction too. All silver and gold, and every vessel of bronze and iron are holy to the Lord. They shall go into the treasury of the Lord."

They shouted a great shout, and the walls all around Jericho fell before them. The armed men went into the city and did as Joshua commanded. The young men who spied inside Jericho days before this went into the city and got the prostitute Rahab and all her family out safely just like they promised her after she hid them. Her faith in God saved Rahab. Rahab was later listed in the genealogy of Jesus. Then the city was burnt up, never to be rebuilt ever again.

Joshua and the people trusted God even if His commands made no sense to the reason of human thinking. The relationship between Joshua, the Hebrews, and God was stable at this moment. Joshua trusted God, and the Hebrews trusted God. God showed them that He knows what He is doing. The result of this trust was, He gave them victory. The more they trusted, the more they got to know God. The more they knew Him, the more they trusted Him. God trusted Joshua, and the people would obey him. It was a mutual trust.

This kind of trust is true of our relationships with other humans. When we get married, we have a certain level of trust in our spouse.

As we get to know him or her better, the more faith we have or don't have. Trust and knowledge can grow together to strengthen our relationships with each other. Trust and knowledge of God do grow together. It takes time and is a process in all of our relationships. God is worth knowing and trusting. He wants a relationship with you, but it requires that you trust Him in an ongoing relational process.

A question to ponder: It can be challenging to find someone you can trust with all the things you have done and thought. What is it like when we discover that a parent, friend, spouse, etc., can be trusted with who you really are?

8

Honesty Builds Trust
JONAH (JONAH 1–4)

Jonah was a prophet of God, and his contemporaries were Amos and Hosea. Most importantly, Jonah had a good relationship with God.

One day while Jonah was praying and listening for a word from God, he heard something that he didn't want to hear. God told him to go to Nineveh to tell them that the Lord God was going to destroy them because of their evil ways against Him.

Nineveh was not in a relationship with God. Jonah knew they were Israel's ruthless enemy who had done horrible things to the Jews in the past. Jonah expected that they might repent at God's message. In anger and fear, Jonah decided to run, and as a result, he tried to separate himself from God. Jonah packed up and started his journey by ship to Tarshish from Joppa. (*Jonah was kidding himself that he could flee from God when He is everywhere. He was so angry that he couldn't think straight.*)

While aboard the ship, Jonah was feeling pleased with himself. But God wasn't so happy with him and caused a great storm that threatened to break up the ship. The crew threw the cargo overboard to lighten the load in an attempt to be saved. Jonah went down to the inner part of the vessel and fell asleep.

After some discussion, the crew decided to cast lots to see who had caused this threat to them. The lot fell on Jonah, which was no surprise to him. They wanted to know who he was and what he had done. He told them he was a Hebrew, and he fears the God of heaven who created the sea and land. He said to them that he disobeyed God's spoken word and was trying to flee his presence. He was candid with these strangers by confessing the truth.

They asked, "What shall we do?"

Jonah told them to throw him overboard so the sea would become calm. But they disobeyed and tried to row harder and harder to get back to land. The sea became even wilder. It was way too hard. They begged God not to punish them because they were innocent, and they were willing to please Him by making a sacrifice and making vows to the Lord God. (*This was more than Jonah was willing to do.*)

Then they threw Jonah into the sea. The ship was out of danger now. Their honesty and obedience saved them.

The Lord, in His mercy and love for Jonah, had a great fish swallow him up. He was in the belly of this fish for three days and nights. There Jonah prayed a heartfelt prayer, knowing the character of God, who is merciful, steadfast loving, and good. Jonah knew he should be dead, but God spared him. He prayed for God's help, knowing he was wrong and there were consequences to his rebellion. God saved him, and Jonah was now willing to yield to God's will.

He turned from his selfish heart to an obedient heart. Jonah made an honest prayer, and God heard him. Honesty strengthens relationships. God had the giant fish vomit Jonah out onto dry land. This news spread to many countries, including Nineveh.

God repeated his command to go to Nineveh and tell the people what the Lord told him. Jonah went because of God's words. It was a three-day journey. When he got there, even though his heart wasn't truly in it, he proclaimed to the people, "In forty days, Nineveh will be destroyed."

Jonah knew what was going to happen. They believed what God had said and called for a fast and put sackcloth and ashes on their heads as a sign of true repentance. The king joined the people and repented of his ways. One would have thought that Jonah would have been thrilled that these dangerous enemies had turned to God, but he wasn't. Instead, he had some unhealed anger in him.

Now Jonah prayed another honest prayer to God, "O Lord, is this not what I said when I was in Jerusalem? That is why I went as fast as I could to Tarshish for I knew you so well that You are gracious and merciful, slow to anger, and have a steadfast love and can change your mind when heartfelt repentance takes place. Therefore, since I am not getting my way, please, it is better for me to die than to live." Finally, Jonah is honest with God instead of running away.

God's response was this: "You need to examine your heart to see why you are so angry and not joyful at this news."

With no intention of examining himself, Jonah left the city for a favorable spot to view what was going to happen to Nineveh. He was still hoping God would destroy this evil place and people.

He made a booth for himself to have some shade from the hot sun. Now, God grew a plant with large leaves to shade Jonah and to prevent him from becoming faint from the hot sun. Jonah knew where it came from and was delighted. But God's lesson wasn't over. He appointed a worm to eat this plant at night and caused a scorching east wind to blow on him the next day. (*God turned up the heat, so to speak.*)

It got so bad, Jonah called out again, "It would be better that I die."

This statement is another honest one by Jonah. God wanted him to have compassion and empathy for what it is like to be helpless and hopeless, like the people of Nineveh who needed to be saved.

God responded, "Did you not feel pity for the plant that you didn't create and grow and was taken away at night? And should I not pity the people of Nineveh who are like little children and don't know any better how to live without knowing me?"

This is another honest statement by God to Jonah. Honesty builds trust in a relationship. God's truthfulness shows how much He wants a relationship with both Jonah and the people of Nineveh.

To be in a relationship with God, we must be honest with Him like Jonah was at times. We can be angry and free to complain to Him. He is a great listener and can save us from ourselves. Relationships grow stronger when honesty is the norm rather than the exception. God is honest with us; in the same way He reached out to have a relationship with Jonah, we must be frank and open with Him too. We must tell God that we are the ones who run from the relationship by our rebellion against Him. Like Nineveh, we must repent.

God had a love for Jonah and wanted him to repent after he disobeyed Him. God showed his love both for a prophet and the sinful people of Nineveh, who were terrorists. But both must be honest with themselves, and God and repent of their sins. God was a patient teacher to Jonah because of His great desire to have a healthy relationship with him. God never gave up and actively pursued Jonah and the people of Nineveh.

You need to be honest with both yourself and God about how you broke the relationship and your heartfelt desire to be reconciled with Him.

A question to ponder: What is it like to be honest with someone? Explain how you felt and what happened.

9

The Lord Looks at the Heart
David (1 Samuel 15–17, Psalm 23, and 2 Samuel 11–12)

The story of David begins with God anointing Saul to be the first king of Israel. He was a good king until the Lord ordered him to go and destroy all the sinful Amalekites and all they possessed. Saul did not obey this order and saved their king and some of the sheep and oxen for a sacrifice to God. (*It sounds like a good thing to do, but it was disobedient.*)

God tells the prophet Samuel to go to Saul and confront him about his rebellious heart and tell him how the Lord feels about this. Samuel does this. But Saul makes some excuse for why he did not obey and takes no responsibility for it and blames the people. To which Samuel responds,

> Has the Lord as great delight in burnt offerings and sacrifices, as in obeying the voice of the Lord?

Behold, to obey is better than sacrifice, and
to listen than the fat of rams.

For rebellion is as the sin of divination, and
presumption is as iniquity and idolatry.

Because you have rejected the word of the
Lord, He has also rejected you from being king.
(1 Sam. 15:22–23)

Saul admitted he obeyed the people rather than God, and he
wanted to be forgiven. God knew his wicked heart by loving his
power and not loving Him. Samuel said, "No, the Lord has someone
better in mind."

The Lord had a plan. He wanted one of Jesse's boys to be the
next king. Samuel was sent to Jesse in Bethlehem with a heifer to
make a sacrifice. When Samuel arrived, he went to the elders and
told them that he was there in peace and to make a sacrifice. Samuel
asked them to dedicate themselves and join him in the offering to the
Lord. When Jesse and the boys came, Samuel immediately spotted
Jesse's son Eliab and thought to himself, "Surely this is the one to be
anointed."

But the Lord said to Samuel, "Do not look at his appearance
or his physical stature because I have refused him. For the Lord does
not see as man sees, for man looks at the outward appearance, but the
Lord looks at the heart" (1 Sam. 16:7).

Jesse then presented each of the other sons one by one to
Samuel, who rejected them all. Samuel then asked Jesse, "Are all your
sons here?"

Jesse replied, "No, the youngest is tending to the sheep."

"Bring him here, and we will wait until he gets here."

David was ruddy looking with bright eyes and good looking. The Lord told Samuel to go and anoint David. He took out the horn of oil and anointed him in front of the rest of the family. The Spirit of the Lord came upon David from that day forward. David was and continued to be very spiritual but not perfect. God knew David had a heart for Him.

David has been recognized as the author of many of the psalms or songs that expressed his understanding and love for God. They were used for worship by David and others. The most famous one is Psalm 23:

> The Lord is my shepherd; I shall not want.
> He makes me lie down in green pastures.
> He leads me beside still waters.
> He restores my soul.
> He leads me in the paths of righteousness for His
>   name's sake.
> Even though I walk through the valley of the
>   shadow of death,
> I will fear no evil,
> For You are with me;
> Your rod and Your staff, they comfort me.
> You prepare a table before me in the presence of
>   my enemies;
> You anoint my head with oil;
> My cup overflows.
> Surely goodness and mercy shall follow me all the
>   days of my life,
> And I shall dwell in the house of the Lord forever.
>   (Ps. 23:1–6)

One example of David's heart being for the Lord was a story that led David's heart away from the Lord. One day David was looking out onto the city, and he saw a beautiful naked woman. Her name was Bathsheba. His lust for her was intense. He had to have her and made sure he did. Shortly afterward, she told him that she was pregnant. This news was a grave problem for the king.

David planned to have her husband, his friend, return from the war and encouraged him to spend time with his wife before he went back to fighting for his country. This way, David would not be caught in his adulterous affair. But the husband would have no part in David's hopeful plan. He could never do it while his men were suffering in battle. David then arranged secretly to have him put on the front line, and it wasn't long before he was killed. David quickly took Bathsheba as a wife. Now he was free to go on as king with no stains on his record.

But God had Nathan, another friend, confront David's blindness to his sins. He told David a story about a rich man who took a poor man's only sheep to be used to feed a guest. When the story was over, David expressed his strong feelings about this injustice and what should be done to this evil man. Nathan's next words struck David's heart to the core.

Nathan said, "You are the man!"

He realized what he had done to God and turned his heart back to the Lord by repenting. Nathan said, "Even though you deserve to die, by God's grace, you will not, but there are always consequences to doing evil against the Lord." David wrote about his rebellion, became humbler, and worshipped God with more heart than he did in the past.

God wanted David's heart completely, and He wants our hearts to be focused on Him too. Like David, we will not do this perfectly;

but when we mess up, then we always need to return our hearts to the Lord. You might ask why God had David become the king when he disobeyed God's word and did such horrible sins. David was the king by which all other kings were measured, but God had a plan for a perfect king who is the King of all kings. This king is Jesus Christ who reigns over the kingdom of God. He was promised to be and is a descendant of David.

Questions to ponder: Has anyone like Nathan pointed out a wrong and you knew he or she was right? What did you do to resolve the wrong?

10

Be Mad at Him
Naomi (Book of Ruth)

This story begins surprisingly. Elimelech took his wife, Naomi, and his two sons to Moab because of a famine in Bethlehem. It appears that no one else in Bethlehem did the same. However, when you are hungry, you are willing to go to any country, even an enemy's. Moab was an enemy of Israel. King Balak of Moab had oppressed them around this time.

Elimelech died there, and his two sons, Mahlon and Chilion, married Moabite women. The wives' names were Orpah and Ruth. Moabites were pagans who worshiped idols, and it was against Jewish law for them to have married such women. But they did it anyway. After remaining there ten years, the two sons died.

After hearing Bethlehem now had food, Naomi decided to return home. All the women were in a period of heavy grieving. This meant that they said and did things they wouldn't usually say and do.

Naomi said, "Return to your family, and the Lord God will bless you because you have been so good to our family and loyal to me. You are young and can get married again. I can't provide a husband for you, so go." They insisted on going with Naomi. She responded by stating, "The Lord has gone against me, so you should not go with me. Return to your gods."

They cried deeply and loud. Orpah kissed Naomi goodbye, but Ruth held tightly to Naomi's legs. She wasn't about to let go.

"See, Orpah is smart by going. You need to go also," Naomi said.

"Stop trying to persuade me to return," Ruth said. "Where you go, I will go, where you lodge, I will lodge. Your people shall be my people, and your God shall be my God. Where you die, I will die, and there I will be buried. By my vow to the Lord, only death will separate me from you." (*No question she was going with Naomi. The conversation was over, and Ruth won.*)

When they arrived in Bethlehem, the whole town was excited. One woman asked, "Is this Naomi?"

She responded, "Don't call me Naomi anymore. Instead, call me Mara ['bitter'], for the Lord Almighty has been very awful to me. I left here well, and the Lord has brought me back totally broke, broken, and bitter. Almighty God has brought calamity upon me. I am furious, and I don't understand why He has done this to me."

The two women found a place to stay, and while there, Naomi mentioned that in town, she had a relative of her husband, a worthy man named Boaz. He owned land and was having his barley cut and collected. Since they had no food, Ruth said she would go and pick up the stalks left after the first cutting on his land. This was allowed by the law so the poor could be fed. Naomi told her to go. It was a great plan, but Ruth had no idea where his land was. So she began working in the first field that she entered. As she worked, she unknowingly crossed over into a field that Boaz owned.

Boaz happened to come to this field that day to inspect the reaping of his barley. (*Was this a coincidence or a God-incidence?*) He greeted the workers, "The Lord be with you." They responded, "The Lord bless you." Ruth's beauty caught Boaz's eye, and he asked, "Whose young woman is this?"

The young man in charge told him about this Moabite woman who had come back with Naomi and how hard she worked to glean the stalks.

Boaz spoke to Ruth, calling her "daughter" because she was young enough to be his, telling her not to glean anywhere else, saying, "You can come here as long as we have grain. I have reminded the young men not to touch you in any way. Feel free to drink from the vessels that the young men have drawn."

Not knowing who he was, she fell on her face, asking why he was so gracious to a foreigner.

He replied, "Word has gotten around Bethlehem about how you sacrificed by leaving everything and everyone to be a friend and companion to Naomi and a follower of our God. May the Lord repay you for what you have done, and may the Lord, the God of Israel, under whose wings you have come to take refuge, give you a full reward."

"Thank you for treating me like one of your servants, which I am not" was her reply.

When it was time to eat dinner, Boaz told her she could have bread to dip in the wine and gave her some roasted grain. She ate until she was full and had leftovers. As Ruth was leaving, he told her and the young men to let her gather up stalks from the stalks they had tied together to move to the threshing floor. She worked until evening, and she beat grain from the stalks she had put together for

Naomi and herself. It was about thirty to forty pounds of grain. That was a lot to carry. (*She had to be very strong.*)

Ruth brought the grain and leftovers home. When Naomi saw what she had gleaned, she was moved deeply by the Spirit of God, reminding her of His love and mercy for her. She felt truly blessed by what He had done for her.

Naomi was moving from bitterness to blessedness. She recognized that God was her hope. Ruth gave her the leftovers for her evening meal. When Naomi heard that she ended up in Boaz's field, she prayed, "May he be blessed by the Lord whose kindness has not forsaken the living and the dead."

Naomi went on to explain to Ruth that Boaz was a potential redeemer who might be able to save them from their plot in life. She encouraged Ruth to continue working in Boaz's field. Naomi then instructed how a young woman can make it known to a man that she is open to marrying him decently and respectably.

Ruth washed up, anointed herself with oil, and put her cloak over her head before heading to the threshing floor where Boaz would be. She watched and saw that he was full and lay down to sleep. She then went to him and uncovered his feet, as she was instructed, and lay down at his feet.

At midnight, Boaz awoke, startled to see a woman at his feet. He asked, "Who are you?"

She replied, "I am Ruth, your servant. I have been told that you are a redeemer."

"Yes, I am, but there is one who is before me," Boaz said. "I will go tomorrow to town to find out if he wants to redeem you. If not, I will, as the Lord leads."

They both went back to sleep until the morning when she went home very quietly. Boaz gave her a large portion of grain to take with her. She arrives at home with the grain and told Naomi everything. They now had to wait for the matter to be resolved.

Boaz went to town the next day and sat by the gate where village decisions and judgments were made, waiting for the other redeemer to show up. When he came, Boaz requested that he sit down next to him. Boaz went and found ten elders because it was needed to make a legal agreement. Boaz told him that Naomi was selling her property, and he was the first redeemer. At first, he said yes; but when Boaz said to him that it comes with Ruth, the Moabite daughter-in-law, he said, "No, because I don't want my inheritance to possibly be split between my children and any children born of Ruth." This rejection freed up Boaz to marry Ruth.

They got married, and they had a son named Obed, the father of Jesse, who was the father of King David. This is the line of the Messiah, Jesus, who was born in Bethlehem.

Naomi and Ruth were now safe and secure. Naomi saw God's plan for her, even though it was tough to suffer the losses of her husband and sons. He provided for her a loving and loyal daughter-in-law, who was a blessing to her, and a redeemer who helped save her. God is good and knows what He is doing by having a plan.

We too will have ups and downs in our relationships with God because we are sinful human beings. We will get mad at Him at times, but we need to learn to wait like Naomi to see God's plan for us to play out. And Ruth also was later included in the genealogy of Jesus.

Questions to ponder: Have you ever had a friend or have been a friend like Ruth was to Naomi? How did that feel?

11

The Lord's Steadfast Love
Job (Book of Job)

The Book of Job is one of the Wisdom books to guide us in understanding God and how to live life the best way, even when it is painful. The book begins with a discussion between Satan and God, which is a shock to readers. Satan tries to convince God that Job's trust and worship of Him were self-centered. He thought that Job's willingness was driven from being blessed. This was supposed to be the basis for the relationship. Satan wants to test his opinion, so God allows him to do it. But he is not allowed to kill Job. God was in charge and put boundaries on Satan. This book never answers the questions of why evil exists in the world and why God allows suffering and harm to happen even to faithful believers.

Satan killed Job's children, took his possessions, and inflicted painful physical suffering like sores all over his body. Of course, Job, being human, grieves heavily for his losses. Grieving is necessary, natural, and a normal part of humanity.

Three of his friends come to console him and encourage him in his grief. His friends were wisdom teachers, so they tried to apply their wisdom to get Job to shape up. The names of his friends were Eliphaz, Bildad, and Zophar. (*You won't find these names in the modern book of baby names for boys.*)

The wisdom of the day, as expressed in other parts of the Old Testament, was that if you suffered, then you must have sinned against God; conversely, if you were blessed, then you must have pleased God by your efforts. God corrects this belief in this story! Jesus also debunked this kind of thinking when he was asked about the blind man. "Did his parents sin, or did the man's sin cause his blindness?" Jesus was asked. "Neither," Jesus said. "He is blind for my purpose to heal him, so people will know who I am." The sole cause of suffering isn't sinning against God.

Considering themselves to be wise, his three friends tried to convince him to be honest with himself and confess his major sins to God. The problem was that Job hadn't committed any major sins, so he felt that he didn't deserve all this suffering. He kept defending his integrity after each, one by one, kept hammering away at Job with their nonwisdom or stupidity. (*With friends like these three, who needs enemies?*)

Besides all his friends challenging his integrity, after all the couple's losses, his wife provided a piece of broken pottery to scrape his sores. She then said to Job, "Curse God and die." She challenged both Job's and God's integrity. Let's remember, she was also depressed from these unthinkable, significant losses.

Another friend, Elihu, had come to visit and advise Job with the three friends but waited to speak because he was younger. He felt his three wise friends had not helped Job. He didn't like Job's self-righteous attitude. He believed God was just, so His punishment must be just. Job needed to accept his punishment as fair and move on. Job wanted to present his case to God or an arbitrator. Elihu replied that God didn't need to hear his case because God already knows the truth about Job.

To Job's surprise, God spoke to him through a storm. He didn't answer all of Job's demands and questions about his suffering but instead raised His questions.

God asked Job a series of questions: "Where were you when I laid the foundations of the earth? Who established the morning dawn? Has the rain a father? Do you know when the mountain goats give birth? Did you decide to have the eagle build its nest up high?"

The Lord reminded Job that He never acts out of character. Instead, God questioned Job on where the power came from to create the universe and galaxies and to maintain them. He also asked him about his wisdom to appear before Him to present his case like a clever lawyer who depends on his skills. God said, "There is no one on earth that is like me."

Now how could Job defend his false and unwise position before God?

After listening to God's questions, Job had second thoughts. He acknowledged his lack of knowledge and understanding: "I'm convinced: You can do anything and everything. Nothing and no one can upset your plans. You asked, 'Who is this muddying the water, ignorantly confusing the issue, second-guessing my purposes?' I admit it. I was the one. I babbled on about things far beyond me, made small talk about wonders way over my head. I'm sorry—forgive me. I'll never do that again. I promise!" (*The Message* by Eugene Peterson).

God rebukes Job's friends for promoting the false belief about suffering and blessing. God encouraged Job to pray for his friends to restore their relationship. He did.

God gave him more possessions than he initially lost and blessed him with even more children. God's love was steadfast through all of Job's complaints. He truly loved Job and had great faith in him, knowing he would prove Satan wrong. In his Psalms, David speaks many times about how he very much appreciated God's steadfast love and faithfulness.

Even though we suffer in life, it doesn't mean that God is not good and He doesn't know what He is doing. It doesn't mean that He hates us or that He is punishing us. He loves all of us and keeps on loving us.

A question to ponder: Steadfast love for another is impossible to find in a human. What is it like to have someone deeply love you over time, especially if you don't always deserve it?

12

God of Restoration
Peter (Four Gospel Books)

One beautiful day John the Baptist was standing with Andrew and another one of his disciples. Jesus walked by, and John said, "Behold, the Lamb of God!"

Andrew was moved by these words and, along with the other disciple, followed behind Jesus. Jesus stopped and asked them, "What are you seeking?" They wanted to spend time with him, so they wanted to know where he was going to spend the night. They went with him and talked all night.

The next day, Andrew went home and told his brother Simon that they had made an extraordinary discovery. God had revealed to them who the Messiah was. Andrew and Simon went to talk to Jesus so Simon would know the truth too. Later, Jesus was to call Simon "Peter," which means "rock." *(Why did Jesus do that?)*

Sometime later, perhaps as soon as the next day, Jesus was walking by the Sea of Galilee. He saw Peter and Andrew casting out their nets into the sea, for they were fishermen. Jesus said to them, "Come and join me as my disciples."

They dropped everything and left the area with James and John, who were also fishermen and were invited by Jesus. (*Their fathers must have been very unhappy unless their sons had told them that Jesus was the Messiah and that following him was more important than fishing.*)

Peter was indeed a character. No one ever knew what he was going to say and do while with Jesus for three years. Sometimes he was impulsive like when he went up the mountain with Jesus and James and John. There they witnessed an amazing scene—Jesus's face shone like the sun, and his clothes became as white as light. Then Moses (who represented the law) and Elijah (who represented the prophets) were talking to him. Peter immediately told Jesus they would make three tents for them if he wished.

As he was still speaking, they heard a loud voice from a cloud, "This is my beloved Son with whom I am well pleased. Listen to him." When Peter and the others heard this, they fell on their faces and were terrified. Jesus came and touched them, saying, "Rise, and have no fear." And when they lifted their eyes, they saw no one but Jesus back in his normal state.

He had passionate opinions, which he expressed strongly, but were often wrong. At what is known as the Last Supper, on Thursday before Jesus was crucified, Jesus began washing the feet of the disciples to show them that he was a servant and they would need to become servants too. Washing of feet was done by servants and usually done when a visitor came into one's house. This was the proper thing to do.

When Jesus came to Peter for the foot washing, he vehemently objected to Jesus. Jesus replied, "What I am doing, you do not understand, but after my work here is finished, you will understand." He also said, "If I don't wash you, you will not be in a lasting relationship with me." Peter then said that Jesus could wash his feet, hands, and head. Jesus answered him, "You are clean except for your filthy feet." Jesus washed his feet.

To be fair, Peter was also right at times and had great wisdom from listening to Jesus. Many of the hundreds of disciples of Jesus left him after they were taught some hard principles. Jesus then turned to the twelve and asked, "Do you want to go away too?"

Peter piped up right away, "Lord, to whom shall we go? You have the words of eternal life, and we have believed and have come to know that you are the Holy One of God."

But Peter was very human, as you can see. One of his human instincts was to stay alive. After Jesus was arrested by a band of soldiers and officers from the chief priest and the Pharisees, Peter followed Jesus, along with another disciple. The other disciple went into the court where Jesus could be seen and got a servant girl, who kept watch of the door, to let Peter come into the court.

She asked, "Aren't you one of the disciples of the man arrested?"

Peter replied, "No, I am not one of them!"

Like many, Peter went to the fire to warm himself because it was a cold evening. A group standing by the fire asked him, "Are you one of his disciples?"

"No, I am not."

Another servant who was in the garden asked, "Didn't I see you in the garden?"

For the third time, he denied it, and the rooster crowed. Peter sobbed like a father who had just lost a child. This is significant because at the Last Supper, Jesus told Peter that he would deny Him three times before the rooster crowed. Right before this, Peter said that he would die for Jesus. Jesus was correct.

Was this the end of Peter as a disciple? No, it was not. Jesus did a very merciful and gracious thing for Peter. After Jesus's resurrection, he met with the disciples several times; and during one of the last times in Galilee, after they had finished breakfast, Jesus met with Peter privately.

Jesus asked, "Do you love me?"

Peter once again spoke forcefully, "You know that I love you!"

Jesus said, "Feed my lambs."

Jesus asked a second time, "Do you love me?"

"Yes, you know I love you!"

Jesus replies, "Tend to my sheep."

He wasn't through yet because he asked a third time to match the three denials. "Do you love me?"

"Lord, you know everything, including my heart, so you know that I love you deeply."

Jesus replied, "Feed my sheep."

All was well between Jesus and Peter.

From that day forward, Peter became the natural leader of this new religion called Christianity. He gave the sermon at the Jewish festival Pentecost after the Holy Spirit arrived just as Jesus had promised. There where thousands of men who came to trust in Jesus Christ that day. Peter went from being a coward to becoming an essential leader of the church where it grew all over the known world in a relatively short period.

God had a plan and purpose for Peter. The Lord used Peter's gifts and his weaknesses to help him grow in the process of trusting in Jesus Christ. God had him and others lead and spread this Good News, which God had them sent to teach to the world. God is still doing this today. His God-given purpose is why Simon's name was changed to Peter, which means "rock," because of this faith and selected position of leader of the church.

A question to ponder: What meaning for your name would you like?

13

The Greatest Conversion of All Time
PAUL (ACTS AND PAUL'S LETTERS TO CHURCHES)

When the apostles began spreading the news about Jesus being the Messiah and his resurrection, the opponents tried to say they were making the whole thing up and that they had false teachings. As we know, the apostles died while boldly standing firm to the truth. They followed Jesus to the grave. This is why Paul's story is so compelling to support what the apostles were preaching and teaching. For me, his story—along with God always keeping his promises in the history of Israel—and the truths about Jesus put away any doubts about whether scripture is true. Paul turned from being Jesus's enemy to becoming the most ardent supporter and teacher of the Gospel.

Paul doesn't show up in the Gospels but shows up in the Book of Acts, which is the story of the early formation of the church in Israel and the known world. Paul was his Roman name, and Saul was his Hebrew name.

The deacon Stephen preached the Good News of Christ in the streets of Jerusalem. The Jewish religious and political leaders were selfishly concerned about losing their power and benefits that the

Romans had given them. Any disruption could put an end to their favor. Stephen's disruption cost him his life. As one of these leaders, Saul approved of this execution. This murder was the beginning of great persecution of the church in Jerusalem. Saul would go from house to house and drag out Christians and have them put in jail or sometimes death.

Saul continued his pursuit of Christians by asking for letters from the high priest so he could go to the synagogues in Damascus to look for any men and women who were part of the Way. This was the name Christians gave themselves because Jesus is the True Way to God. Saul proceeded to Damascus with a small band of helpers. As he approached Damascus, suddenly, a bright light shone around him; and Saul fell to the ground in shock and surprise. A bigger surprise would come next.

He heard a voice say to him, "Saul, Saul, why are you persecuting me?"

Saul asked, "Who are you?"

The voice replied, "I am Jesus whom you have been persecuting. But rise and enter the city, and you will be told what to do."

The men with Saul heard the voice but did not see anyone speaking. Saul rose from the ground, and even though his eyes were open, he could not see a thing. His men led him to Damascus where he didn't eat or drink for three days. (*Wow, can you imagine God entering into your life this way?*)

In a vision, the Lord told a disciple of Christ called Ananias to go to the house of Judas on the street of Straight and find a man named Saul. Likewise, Saul will see in a vision, as he was praying, a man coming to restore his eyesight.

Ananias was shocked because he had heard about the evil Saul had committed by destroying the saints, even though there was no proof that Saul himself had killed anyone. He had heard that Saul was in Damascus to do the same to the saints there. In the vision, Jesus said, "Go, for he is a chosen instrument of mine to carry my Name before the Gentiles and kings and the children of Israel. I will show him how much he must suffer for the sake of my name." (*Interestingly, Saul must suffer too even though a chosen one of God.*)

Ananias obediently went to Saul and laid hands on him and told him that his sight would be restored and he would be filled with the Holy Spirit like the apostles. All this happened. Saul arose and was baptized. He then ate and drank to regain his strength.

Saul spent several days listening to the disciples in Damascus and asking questions. In the synagogues, Saul began preaching that Jesus is the Son of God and proving to the Jews that Jesus is the Christ. They too were shocked at what Saul was doing. They were fearful that Saul was tricking them into capturing and putting them in jail.

Other Jews at that time were not convinced of Saul's conversion, so they plotted to kill him. This plot became known to Saul, and the disciples helped him escape through an opening in the wall in a basket.

Eventually, he went to Jerusalem to meet the apostles. They were skeptical at first but came around to the truth that Jesus mystically converted him. Paul went on to become the greatest missionary of all time. He made three long and fruitful trips and started many churches of believers along the way. One of the things Paul taught was that by the death of Christ, who took on all of our sins, Jesus reconciled us to God.

God protected him from death many times, but he was arrested and was eventually martyred by the Romans, leaving a great legacy that affects millions of people today. Paul didn't ask for his calling, but God planned it for this purpose. God has a plan and purpose for everyone, but not everyone is willing to receive His gift of salvation and a new creation. They will never know what their real purpose for being born is.

Questions to ponder: Have you ever felt like God could never forgive you for what you did? We are told that all of our sins are forgiven. *All* means "all," not "most of my sins." How do you now feel about being forgiven by God?

14

Deep Love
Two Lost Sons (Luke 15)

J esus tells three stories that are called parables, which are short stories with a moral lesson at the end. The third one is a parable about a father and two of his sons.

The story began with the youngest son meeting privately with his father and asking for his inheritance. His portion by Jewish law was one-third of the entire estate. The oldest son would get two-thirds at the father's death. But the father wasn't dead, so the son is saying to his father, "I wish you were dead." This idea would have been considered a very shameful thing for the son to say and do. Why, we don't know, but the father cashed out a third of his property and gave it to his rebellious son. Off he went to the closest large city in a far country. There he tries to impress his new friends and has some wild parties.

Eventually, the money ran out, and his new friends abruptly said goodbye. A famine came upon this country, and the poor boy had to find work to eat. He got a job that required him to go into the field and feed the pigs. Well, for a Jew, a pig was considered unclean, and this would have been frowned upon, to say the least. No one gave him any food. Some think he took some of the pigs' food. (*Wow, he was at the bottom of the pit.*)

As he reflected on his decision to leave his father, he realized that his father's servants had more than enough food to eat. He decided to return home.

We don't know how long he was gone—a month, six months, or two years—we simply don't know because it never says. But as his son reached the horizon of his father's land, the father spotted him coming. The father must have checked every day, hoping his son would return. The father ran as fast as he could to get to his lost son. Dust was flying up all over the place from his scandals. He didn't care. When he reached his son, out of compassion and love, he hugged and kissed him.

The son spoke as soon as he could after the father eased his hug, "Father, I have sinned against heaven and you. I am no longer worthy of being called your son. Please treat me as one of your hired servants."

The father said to his servants as they got close to the house, "Bring him the best robe and put a ring on his hand and shoes on his feet as quickly as you can. Get the best calf we have and let us eat and celebrate. My son was dead and now is alive and was lost, but now he is found." They began to celebrate.

His older brother was in the field working, and when he was done, he walked toward the house and heard all the music and dancing. He asked the first servant he saw, "What is the celebration for because it is not a special holiday?"

The servant said, "Your brother has come home, and your father was so excited that he decided to throw a party to celebrate his safe return."

He became angry at these words, and he refused to join the celebration. His father noticed this and came out to his son. The son angrily said, "Father, I have stayed with you all these many years and served you. I never disobeyed your commands. You never celebrated me with my friends. When this son of yours, who was reckless with your property and lived a wild lifestyle to shame you and me, comes home, you are so excited that you throw this outrageous party."

His father replied, "Yes, I appreciate your commitment to me all these years, and all that I have is yours. [In other words, the younger son isn't going to get any more inheritance.] It is fitting to celebrate and be glad for your brother was dead and now is alive and lost and now is found."

The moral is that the father represents God who had a love for His two boys. Both rebelled against their father. The youngest son's rebellion is obvious, but even though the older one stayed home, he rejected the father's invitation to have compassion and love for his younger brother by celebrating. The elder son is much like Jonah by not being able to celebrate the turning from rebellion back to God. Both sons were lost with the younger being in the past and the older son being in the present.

God loves you too, even though you have rebelled in the past and present. He is waiting for you to return. Believe me, He will throw a party in heaven with great gladness for your return to Him.

A question to ponder: Which character are you in this story? Why?

15

Looking for Love in the Wrong Person
WOMAN AT THE WELL (JOHN 4)

A woman from Samaria went to the well a mile away from town at noon. This meant that she was an outcast in her town. Women would all go to draw water at the coolest times of the day like early morning and early evening. The well was an opportunity for women to talk and share. It was a unique social time for the women of the town. When she arrived all alone, Jesus was there by himself. The disciples had gone to town to buy some food.

He asked her, "Give me a drink."

She was surprised that a Jew asked her for help because the Samaritans (Jews who married Gentiles) and Jews hated each other. She was also surprised that a man would speak to her in a public place. It was well known that talking to a woman was against all social norms of the day. She just stood there staring at him and asked why.

He responded, "If you knew the gift of God and who it is that is asking 'Give me a drink,' you would have asked him, and he would have given you living water."

Jesus used the term *living water* to signify that he would provide for her a transformed spiritual life.

Confused by what he was offering her, she stated that he didn't have anything to draw the water and the well was very deep. She then asked, "Where do you get this fresh, cold water that usually comes from mountain streams?"

"You are now saying that you are greater than our father Jacob, who gave us this well, and he and his family drank from this well," Jesus answered her with a spiritual promise. "Everyone who drinks of this physical water will be thirsty again. The water I give will become a spring of water welling up to eternal life."

She didn't get this, so she said, "Sir, give me this water so that I will not be thirsty and not have to come to this far place to carry fifty pounds of water each day."

Jesus said to her, "Go and get your husband and come back."

"But I have no husband."

Jesus answered, "You are honest when you say that you have no husband, for you have had five husbands and currently living with a man who is not your husband."

"Sir, I perceive that you are a prophet." Now she wanted to change the subject by talking spirituality too. "Our fathers worshipped on this mountain, but the Jews say that Jerusalem ought to be the place to worship God."

Jesus replied, "Woman, believe me, the time is coming when neither on this mountain nor in Jerusalem will you worship the Father. You worship what you do not know and we worship what we know, for salvation will come through the nation of Israel. The time is now when true worshipers will worship the Father in spirit and truth, for the Father is seeking people who will do this."

The woman said, "I know the Messiah who is called the Christ is coming. When he comes, he will tell us all things."

Jesus said to her, "I who speak to you am he."

The disciples returned from town. The outcast woman ran back toward town, leaving her water pot. When she got to town, she said to the people, "Come, see the man who knew all that I have ever done. Can this be the Christ?"

They should have laughed at her, but they saw a glow on her face and joy in her voice. People began walking the mile to see him. Many of the people believed in him because of her testimony. Jesus stayed two days, and many more believed because of his teaching. They believed he was the Savior of the world that was revealed in the first five books of scripture that they kept as part of the Jewish heritage.

She was looking for love from a man, but these five attempts failed. She gave up on marriage and was living with a man. Jesus still loved her and spoke to her about eternal life and a relationship with him whom she could worship in spirit and truth.

Questions to ponder: Are you looking for real, sincere, giving love from an imperfect person? What is this like?

16

Sacrificial Love
JESUS CHRIST'S DEATH AND RESURRECTION (GOSPEL BOOKS)

The Jews were celebrating the Passover feast in Jerusalem. This feast began when the Jews were slaves in Egypt. God told Moses to slay a perfect lamb and put the blood on the doorpost of their homes. This way, God would pass over these homes when He had all the firstborn sons of families living in Egypt killed. God planned to free the Israelites from bondage by having Pharaoh agree to let them leave Egypt, and this is what made it happen.

Jesus and the twelve were celebrating this feast in the room on the second floor of a home. Jesus broke away from the tradition of this meal and instituted the new covenant to the world. (*His words are now used in the Mass, Holy Eucharist, and Holy Communion services around the world by a variety of Christian denominations.*)

Jesus took the bread, blessed it, broke it, and he then said, "Take, eat, this is my body." (*This symbolized the breaking of his body the next day.*) Then Jesus took the cup in his hands, and after he had given thanks to the Father, he gave it to his disciples and said, "Drink it, all of you, for this is my blood of the [new] covenant, which is poured out for many for the forgiveness of sins." (*The wine symbolized his blood like the perfect lamb at Passover to save you and me.*)

Judas afterward left this meal to betray him. Peter was told that he would deny him three times, which he denied that he would ever do.

Jesus leads the disciples after the meal to the Garden of Gethsemane to pray. He asked them to pray while he went to a place alone to pray to the Father. Three times he went to a lonely place and prayed after falling on his face, "My Father, if this cannot pass unless I drink it, your will be done." Knowing the physical and spiritual pain the cross would bring, Jesus was still willing to do it because it was the plan and purpose for him being born by Mary.

Shortly afterward, Judas brought the chief priests and elders and a great crowd carrying swords and clubs. Jesus was arrested without a fight. The disciples left and fled, thinking they might be next. Jesus was taken to Caiaphas, the high priest, where the elders and scribes were waiting.

The temple authorities brought false witnesses against him, but to no avail. Then he was asked if he was the Christ (Messiah). He replied, "You have said so. When you see me next, I will be seated at the right hand of Power and coming on a cloud." (*He is coming back to earth to judge all of humankind.*)

At this, Caiaphas tore his clothes in mourning and said, "He has uttered blasphemy against God."

They shouted, "He deserves death."

He was bound up and dragged to see Pilate because they had no authority to put Jesus to death. Pilate was amazed as Jesus stood in silence during the whole time he was accused and never fought back against the charges. Pilate decided to have the crowd either free

Barabbas or Jesus, as was the tradition. The whipped-up crowd called for the thief Barabbas to be set free. (*A lucky day for him.*) The crowd yelled to Pilate to crucify Jesus over and over again.

Pilate said, "I am innocent of this man's blood." He washed his hands to show that he was innocent in this mess.

The crowd responded to Pilate, "His blood be on our children and us." (*They surely didn't know what they were doing and saying.*)

Jesus was mocked, beaten, and whipped with a tool that had spikes that ripped the flesh wide open on his back. To add insult, they pushed down on his head a crown of two-inch thorns penetrating his skull. Once they arrived at Golgotha, they nailed his feet and wrists to the wooden cross with long, thick spikes. At noon, the cross was hoisted up and securely put into place while he was still on it.

The Jewish religious leaders continued to mock him by these words: "He saved others, yet he cannot save himself" and "Let him come down from the cross, and we will believe in him."

He called to the Father, "Forgive them for they don't know what they are doing." He hung on the cross in pain until three in the afternoon. He said, "It is finished," and then he died. At that time, the sky became dark as far as the eye could see, and the temple curtain was torn down the middle, signifying that believers had direct access to God from now on and not just the chief priest who was in the presence of God in a particular room in the temple. The earth shook like a major earthquake.

Joseph, a Pharisee who believed Jesus, had a burial place; and he and another believing Pharisee wrapped him tightly in cloths once he was taken to Joseph's cave. Then a very heavy stone was rolled over the entrance. The Jewish leaders had placed guards outside the cave so the disciples wouldn't come and take the body and claim he was resurrected. The rock was sealed to prove no one had entered it. He was buried on Friday before the sun went down, which begins the Jewish Sabbath.

The women who followed Jesus went to the tomb on Sunday morning when the Sabbath was over. This was the third day. They had spices and ointments with them to prepare the shrouded body.

Once the three women arrived, they noticed the rock was rolled away, which was a relief since they didn't know how they would enter the tomb. They entered the tomb, ready to go to work, but the body was gone. The look on their faces was one of shock as any of us would be.

Then two angels appeared and asked them, "Why do you seek the living among the dead? He is not here but has risen. Remember how he told you that he would be delivered into the hands of sinful men, crucified, and on the third day rise?"

They remembered and left to tell the eleven and others about what they heard and saw.

That very day, Jesus appeared to two of his disciples as they were traveling to Emmaus. They didn't recognize him until he blessed the bread and wine. He appeared at least three times to the eleven and hundreds of others. Surely, Jesus was the Christ and the Son of God. He kept all His promises.

17

Summary of the Stories

God took the initiative to create humans who are different from all the other creatures. God loves all His creatures but loves humans even more. He gave us the responsibility to watch over and take care of all the rest of creation. As expressed in the creation stories, God wants to be in a relationship with us; as shown by His love, He spent time with Adam and Eve, talking and listening to them. God gave them His very best in the garden. He wanted to be loved in this relationship in return, so He gave them and us the freedom to choose Him or not. With this gift of freedom came the possibility of rejection and evil too. This rejection results in the breaking of the relationship with God. Adam and Eve rejected God's boundaries by accepting the voice of doubt from the serpent. The result was being separated from God in His garden.

As life outside the garden evolved, the rebellion against God got worse, to the point where God wiped out all of creation, except for Noah's family and all the creatures that fit inside the ark. God cared enough to save His creation, especially us.

From this fresh start came a man named Abram who had the gift of faith, which many have come to admire and want. It was uncompromised faith, and it was a maturing faith as his relationship grew. It came to the point where Abraham not only trusted God with his life but with that of his one and only son. He trusted all the promises and covenants that God made with him. He took God at His word. God is very trustworthy. God declared Abraham to be a man worthy of being in a relationship because of his faith in Him.

The sons of Jacob hated their brother Joseph, and they wanted him dead; instead, they sold him to some slave merchants going to Egypt. They never wanted to see him again. But what they meant for evil, God meant for good. Joseph ended up being the mightiest man in Egypt under the pharaoh. God had protected Joseph and gave him gifts that propelled his career. During an extreme famine in that part of the world, Joseph's brothers happened to be forced to go to Egypt because it was known they had plenty of food to sell. Joseph's position had made it possible for all of Jacob's family or the nation of Israel to go to Egypt to be together, survive, and grow for four hundred years. God had a plan for His chosen people and protected them.

While in Egypt, God's nation continued to grow until the pharaoh who knew nothing of Joseph felt threatened and turned the Jewish people into slaves. By His grace, God chose Moses to survive the edict that required all the male baby Jews to be killed. Then Moses was called by God to lead his people out of Egypt and to go back to the Promised Land in Canaan. Again it was by God's grace that Moses, who didn't believe that he had it in him, learned how to lead and grow in faith.

From the story of Joshua who replaced Moses as the leader to take them back to Canaan, we learned that God knows what He is doing. He and the people trusted God with His instructions to defeat the people of Jericho.

Jonah tried to run from God, but God loved him too much to have the relationship end. Jonah knew he couldn't get his way with God and returned to Him by repenting.

David loved God dearly, but his passions lead him away from God for a short period. God loved him too much to let David forget his love for God. Nathan told him a story that brought David's heart back to the reality of what he had done and how it hurt God. What we learn from many of our stories is that God's love can never be permanently separated from the God-committed heart. We must return to Him.

Even though Naomi was very mad at God, it turned out God had a plan for Ruth, who was in the bloodline to Jesus Christ by bearing King David's grandfather. Naomi had lost all her family, except for Ruth, her pagan daughter-in-law. She was very loyal and stayed with her even when the future was unknown. God's grace and mercy saved Naomi and Ruth. Ruth was a model of loyalty that we need to have, to God the Father, through Jesus Christ, and by the Holy Spirit.

Job thought God was very unjust by taking away his children and possessions. His four friends came to comfort him in his grief but ended up alienating him. Job wanted a face-to-face meeting with God to justify his case against what God had done. Instead, God showed up in a storm and asked Job a series of questions that showed how loving and powerful God is. He came to realize that God was sovereign over everything, even allowing his children and animals to die. Job repented of his selfish attitude and self-righteousness. God restored Job's family and possessions, even more than he formerly owned. God trusted Job that he wouldn't give in to Satan's wants.

God's plan to reconcile all the families on the earth, who had faith in God like Abraham, was soon to be revealed at the time the Jewish nation was under Roman rule. Only the trust was to be in the Person of Jesus Christ. God's plan was to give up the life of His one and only Son and have him resurrected.

In this plan, a fisherman named Simon, whose name was changed to Peter, was to become the leader of the original Christians. Peter always had something to say. His eagerness got him into trouble, especially when he denied being a follower of Jesus. Peter's relationship was restored by Jesus, asking him if he loved him three times to equal the three times Peter denied Jesus. What compassion and patience God has with us!

Paul was a staunch opponent of getting rid of Christians by prison or death. He was the most unlikely person to become an apostle of Jesus Christ. But God knew best, and he was converted on his way to Damascus. It was God's grace and initiative that this happened. Paul went from being the enemy of God to His faithful follower who gave his all to Christ. He went on to be a great preacher and teacher of God's word throughout the centuries.

Jesus is an excellent storyteller and told stories to make valuable points. Jesus made many promises about our relationship with God and eternal life with Him. We are to take Jesus at his word. The main point of the lost sons is that God is always hoping you will return to Him, no matter what you have done. God celebrates when you do. He is waiting for you to return to Him.

The "woman at the well" story is one about how a person can be transformed when facing the truth of Jesus, even when an outcast in the eyes of her community. Many in the town were also changed by her witness and their willingness to spend time with Jesus. God's love and truth were greater than the town's judgment of her.

Jesus suffered greatly, but He put us first and ahead of himself. He was willing to die and be separated from the Father for a trillionth of a second or some time to take our sins upon himself to pay the price for our sins. What a great and everlasting gift, but we must receive it by admitting that we broke our relationship with Him and now have a desire to have it restored like Peter and others in the Bible.

Because God loves us so much, He planned to forgive us and wipe our slate clean. He did this by a gift of sacrificing His Son, Jesus Christ, by paying the price for our rebellion, disinterest, etc., and reconciling us to God. We are considered not guilty and viewed by God as being holy like Himself so that we can be part of His family and kingdom. From there, we continue to grow and mature in our faith and relationship.

From these stories and others in scripture, they speak of God wanting a relationship with you. He took the initiative to begin the relationship in these stories. It doesn't matter what you have believed, how mad you are at God, how disappointed you are by the church, or what you have done up to this point in time. God created you for a purpose and has a plan for you because He loves you and loved you, up to this point in time and from the time He had the idea to create you.

His love is called *agape*, which is the highest level of love human-kind can know. It is about putting the other person first. Like the father of the prodigal sons, God is waiting for you to be willing to unite with His desire to have a relationship with you.

The next and last chapter will explain how you can reconcile with God.

18

How to Have a Relationship with God

Why Aren't We in a Personal Relationship with God?

We are not in a relationship with God because we are like Adam and Eve and rebel against God and His boundaries, restrictions, and laws. We want our independence from God. We choose other gods or we want to act like we are God. We want to be in charge of our lives rather than yield to God's grace, mercy, timing, sovereignty, power, and love. We don't want to fulfill God's purpose for our lives. Instead, we want to determine our purpose in life.

We do many things that reject God. We do things that hurt others—lie, put them down, and gossip about them. We are self-centered, selfish, hard-hearted, rebellious, lazy, and self-absorbed. We don't keep God's law or man's law. On top of our inherited sinful nature, we have learned how to make poor choices from the pressure of our culture and environment.

The great tragedy of the twenty-first century is that many people believe that we are good people, have progressed, and don't do anything so horrible to break our relationship with God. This idea is just false and wrong thinking. God tells us in Romans 3:12, "There is no one good, not even one." When we think we are good people, we think good needs to be rewarded and bad needs to be punished. So when we have done bad things, we make excuses or blame others. We just can't face our dark side, which is part of our reality. The truth is, we are all bad and rebel against God and hurt others. We all need Jesus.

We need to be reconciled with God

As a result of being reconciled with God, we receive peace in our souls: We begin to receive wisdom. The hurts and pains begin to heal. Our anger and frustration begin to subside. And our future becomes secure and safe.

We also reveal to the people around us that a relationship with God is important and meaningful. Its power changes us in ways that one could never ever image. Our character and values are transformed so they humbly stand out.

God loves us so much that He gives us a way that we can be reconciled and have an intimate relationship with Him.

God's way to reconciliation

God expresses His reconciling way for us in the following paraphrase of **Ephesians 2** from *The Message* by Eugene H. Peterson:

> Saving is all His idea and all His work. All we do is *trust* [emphasis mine] Him enough to *receive* [*my word*] it. It's God's gift, from start to finish! We don't play a major role. If we did,

we'd probably go around bragging that we'd done the whole thing! No, we neither make nor save ourselves.

Jesus is perfect and thus can be the only one to remove all those things that separates us from God. He does it by his sacrifice on the cross. At the time of His death on the cross, all our unrighteousness was forgiven—past, present, and future. *All* means "all"; there are no exceptions.

The cross also shows us that God takes seriously our acts, thoughts, and attitudes that separate us from Him. He is not blasé about these things and cannot say to us, "You all sin, so let's move on to some other subject and forget our permanent separation!" No, He can't ignore it because of His love for us and His holiness.

The cross is not the end of His way

The Messiah rose from His death so we could have a new beginning of our relationship with the Trinitarian God. His resurrection is confirmation of the gift of forgiveness by symbolizing a fresh start in life. All are invited into this relationship with God the Father, through Jesus Christ, and by the Holy Spirit. Our relationship will be a new and better one, leading us to a perfect relationship after Christ returns to earth at the end-times. Later in our journey, we will learn that God can help us live this new life through the person of the Holy Spirit in power. The resurrection also is confirmation that we will be with God for all eternity.

This Gift Is Offered but Has to Be Received by Us

If I gave a daughter a beautiful diamond ring for Christmas and she was aware of what the gift was but puts it unopened up in her attic, she does not realize the effects and benefits of this gift. This is true of the grace of Jesus's dying and rising from the grave for us. If we don't consent to this gift, the effects and benefits are not realized by us.

The only way we receive this gift is to first repent of our decisions and actions. *Repent* is an interesting word. It means to "turn away *from* something" and then "turn *to* something else in its place." We chose to turn away *from* the ways of the world—our selfishness, trying to earn our relationship with God and turn *to* the right and good ways of God and a reconciled relationship with God as best we can and are capable of doing so with God's help. We are moving toward something better and will like it even more than what we are turning from!

Next, we are to trust our lives in the Savior, Jesus Christ. Jesus is the Savior of our broken relationship with God. Trust is vital in any relationship. Without it, a relationship isn't very intimate and not what it could be.

We express our trust in Christ by communicating with Him by prayer. It doesn't require a special prayer but rather a sincere prayer, acknowledging our desire to be in the best kind of relationship with Him. There is no magic formula or perfectly worded prayer. What is more important is a heartfelt desire and saying to God what is on your heart about your trust in Him. When you do this, you are responding to God's gift. The gift of reconciliation is yours to receive. When we receive God's invitation to the gift of Jesus by faith, we are reconciled to God and put into a relationship with Him forever.

Here is one sample prayer:

God, help me. I have messed up and separated myself from you. I want to accept your gift
of reconciliation by the work of Jesus Christ on
the cross. I desire to give up my ways for Your
ways. I don't know exactly what all this means,
but I am willing to learn and grow. Amen.

Even though you don't have all the answers to your questions or
have the strongest faith at this time, this is the only way God provides
for us to be intimate with Him. Our close relationship with God will
grow from this starting point. It is not only my opinion or my experience but God's faithful promise to us. When we receive God's gift
of Jesus Christ, we can be assured of a relationship with God as His
children and part of His family. Our decision is the beginning of the
relationship and not the end.

Let a pastor or a mature Christian know that you have begun
this new or renewed relationship with God. Find a church because
God intends us to be in communion with other Christians. This is
why the church (all believers) was founded by our Lord and Savior,
Jesus Christ.

ABOUT THE AUTHOR

Bruce Geary is a retired pastor who reflects on the Bible readings as he tries to know God and apply His truths to his life. He said that he learned that Christianity is a process. Members of his Bible studies heard "it is a process" so many times, they kid him about it being on his tombstone.

Once when he was doing his daily quiet time, he said that it felt like a task and that it felt empty. Since he was thinking of writing this book, he asked himself, "Do you really want a relationship with God?" The answer was *yes*, and it changed how he did his quiet time and matured his relationship with the Lord.

CPSIA information can be obtained
at www.ICGtesting.com
Printed in the USA
BVHW050759040821
613579BV00007B/134

9 781644 689479